DY

OF THE

SOUL

TORKOM SARAYDARIAN

T.S.G. Publishing
Foundation, Inc.

Dynamics of the Soul

ISBN: 0-929874-01-3
Library of Congress Card Number: 2001117281

Printed in the United States of America

Cover Design: *Tim Fisher*
Cave Creek, Arizona

Printed by: *Data Reproductions*
Rochester Hills, Michigan

Published by: T.S.G. Publishing Foundation, Inc.
Post Office Box 7068
Cave Creek, Arizona 85327-7068
United States of America
www.tsg-publishing.com

Note: Meditations, visualizations, and other health information are given as guidelines. They should be used with discretion and after receiving professional advice.

Published from donations to the
Torkom Saraydarian Book Publishing Fund

Table of Contents

1

Inner Treasures

Those who have the spirit of gratitude already know that all of Nature, all of Life, is a treasure. We must learn to recognize that everything that exists is a treasure: mountains, rivers, lakes, streams, forests, flowers, birds, animals, minerals, and human beings. All of these are treasures in the treasury of space, and we must relate to them as treasures.

What is a treasure? A treasure is an object, a power, a living being, or a virtue that multiplies and meets your physical, emotional, mental, and spiritual needs. It also becomes a blessing to all around you, and to all those who are far away from you.

When I was four years old, while hiking with my Father in the mountains I saw some people who were driving a carriage with four horses. After watching their joy, I turned to my Father and said, "I do not have a carriage, a horse. . . ." My Father, looking at me, said, "Let us sit on this rock for a moment and I will tell you what you have."

We sat on a rock facing a valley which spread out in front of us for hundreds of miles. "Now, first of all," he said, "you have a nice body. Look at your hands. Here: look at your face in this small mirror. Do you see?"

"Yes."

"Also, all these mountains are yours. The air is yours; the sky is yours; that river is yours. This pure fragrance is yours; these birds are yours. All of this is yours so long as you enjoy and care for these things. And guess what? You also have a father, a mother, sisters, a dog, a few cats. . . ."

"Father," I said, "I did not know that I had all of this."

"Later, when you grow up, you will realize that there are treasures which cannot be seen."

"Can any treasure exist which we cannot see?"

"Yes. For example, your vision is a treasure which you cannot see. Can you see your Mother's love for you?"

"No, but I know that she cares for me."

"Right. There are many treasures in man. One day you will discover them."

I never forgot this talk with my Father, and gradually it sank into my heart. As I grew up I realized that the human being is a great treasure, with his senses, thinking, and creativity. Whenever I walk in the mountains and canyons, it seems to me that I am walking among treasures. A flower, a bush, a bird, a deer is enough to make you feel ecstasy.

Just as a man who lives in luxury feels that all that he has is nothing special, so mankind lives in the treasury of Nature and feels that he has nothing. Unless one realizes that he is a treasure in himself, he cannot see the real treasures in life. The moment he realizes his own worth, he will be filled with gratitude and will become aware of all the treasures by which he is surrounded.

I will never forget the following event. A man and a woman were walking in a field when two horsemen approached the couple, carrying guns. One of them said to the man, "Leave your wife and walk one hundred feet away from her."

"Why? What did I do?"

"We know what you did. Just do as we say if you want your wife to be safe."

In terror, as the man began walking away and as the gunmen took aim, the woman ran and kneeled before the horsemen and in tears cried, "Don't take my treasure from my hands. . . ."

They shot him and rode away. From that day on, I saw my Father, Mother, sisters, uncles, aunts and other relatives as treasures. And I often had a deep fear that they would be taken away.

One day when I was in Father's pharmacy, a young man came to consult with my Father, who was a recognized expert in venereal diseases. The boy was skinny and lifeless. After the consultation, he took the medicine and left. "Father," I said, "what is the matter with him?"

"He wasted his sexual treasures, and also the treasury of his brain — the idiot!"

Later that afternoon I approached a long-time employee of my Father's and confidentially asked him, "Can you tell me about sexual treasures?" He giggled a little, rubbed his long moustache, and in a whisper said, "Where did you hear about that?" "My Father said that the boy who came in this morning had wasted his sexual treasures," I told him. "Well," he said, "if you can keep a secret, I will tell you later."

It took thirty minutes for him to utter just a few words on the subject. As he continued filling prescriptions, he managed to say, "Sexual treasures — I don't know how to tell you because you are so young." "Just tell me!" I demanded. "I am tired of waiting!"

Finally he said, "Well, you know, your organ . . . and the eggs . . . and what comes out at the time one relates with a woman . . . are called treasures. When one gets disease or wastes his treasures through stupidity, he loses his treasures, and —"

"And what?"

"I didn't think you were listening."

I kicked him and went to my Father's office. Since he was busy, I went home. None of the words the pharmacist had spoken were clear in meaning to me, but somewhere in my soul I understood the whole story. The strongest impression was made by the words "wastes his treasures."

In later years when I contemplated about treasures and the treasury, I discovered four facts that made me extremely happy. First, I found out that there were inner, invisible treasures as well as outer and visible treasures. But a more important discovery was that the outer treasures could be increased by investing and sharing them or by using them economically. And inner treasures were also increased by sharing and distributing them with joy and love. The more you gave of your inner treasures, the more you had.

The third discovery was that both the inner and outer treasures do not belong to us but to all life.

The final discovery was that when you share your inner treasures, you not only increase your inner treasures but you also increase your outer treasures. And similarly, when you share your outer treasures with clean motive, you increase your inner treasures.

However, we are taught just the opposite. "Give me, give me, give me — put it right here in my pocket." This is why there are so many poor people in the world while others live luxuriously.

One day while my family was traveling by boat on the ocean I saw a bottle floating in the water. My Mother said, "Can you tell me what that bottle suggests to you?"

"That someone put a cork in it and threw it into the sea."

"Well, that is called a smart escape. But think now. Let me see if you can find something deeper."

The boat sped up and the bottle was left behind. But my mind remained occupied with that bottle. Mother was enjoying the air and the waves of the sea. By the time we reached an island, I still had no answer for her. But after dinner, as Mother and I walked together under some big pine trees, I said, "You know, Mother, a floating bottle is like a foolish man."

"You are very close to finding the answer. Think a little more."

It was back on board that I finally found the answer. "The bottle is in the sea," I said, "but the sea cannot fill it because it is closed."

"Then tell me: who is like this?"

I could not answer. Seeing my agony, she whispered in my ear, "Like those who have abundance but live a poor life."

I kissed Mother and was freed from such pressure. The allegory remained. People live surrounded by treasures, but they feel empty because they are closed. The word "closed" in its connotation was so deep that I was often directed to examine its depth.

What are inner treasures?

In religious literature, I found two towers mentioned. One was the Tower of Babel which was left unfinished because, as their intention was to built "a tower whose top may reach to heaven," the Lord mixed the languages of the workers and they could no longer cooperate with each other.[1] The second tower that impressed me very deeply is the tower that was written about in the Lotus Sutra five hundred years before Christ.

As Lord Buddha was talking to thousands of listeners, He suddenly saw a mighty Tower rise out of the earth. This was called the Treasure Tower.

> At that time there appeared before the Lord Buddha a tower made with seven kinds of precious stones. This tower was four miles high into the sky and it was suspended in mid-air, full of precious objects. . . . Jeweled rosaries hung from the tower; ten thousand million jeweled bells were suspended from its top . . . the most precious fragrances emanated from it. Angels and gods, all singing, serving, worshipping around the Tower. . . .[2]

This description of the Tower fascinated me. These two towers represent

1. A Tower that was decayed, abandoned, and ruined
2. A Tower that emerged from the earth, symbolizing in man all the spiritual treasures a person could have

---

1. Genesis 11:4
2. See *The Threefold Lotus Sutra*, Ch. 11, "Beholding the Precious Stupa."

In the Ageless Wisdom, this Treasure Tower is called the Inner Lotus, or the Chalice, which is hidden within the earth — the body. But slowly, as Its treasures increase, It emerges and blesses the world with Its jewels and treasures.

For billions of years, all the treasures of which you are aware or have experienced are accumulated in that diamond Chalice. Every time you spread Beauty, Goodness, Righteousness, Joy, Freedom, Sacrificial Service, and Gratitude, you deposit jewels in the Chalice.

The essence of all your experiences, which we call wisdom, is accumulated there throughout the ages. The drops of blessing that you receive for every heroic deed you perform to help others are gathered there as pearls.

The essence of all your learning, education, and creative effort is collected there as diamonds.

The drops of inspiration you obtain as a result of aspiration and meditation are all there as rubies.

Curiously enough, whatever you give to others at the expense of your own pleasure and enjoyment is also there, as rare and fragrant oil.

All the labor for others that provides light, love, peace, cooperation, and unity is there as precious incense.

And your treasure house becomes bigger and bigger as you increase in treasure. This is your Tower, which will slowly emerge out of your being, and, like an invisible, fragrant, and fruitful tree, It will share the treasures with all those who can handle treasures.

There are other kinds of treasure. Seventy-seven jewels are formed in the Chalice as the human soul liberates himself. These jewels are virtues — powers — which shine like the rays of the sun and add glory to the human soul.

This treasury was recognized by Christ, Who often spoke of it:

"Stop storing up treasures for yourself upon the earth, where moth and rust consume and where thieves break in and steal. Rather, store up treasures for yourselves in heaven, where neither moth nor rust consumes, and where thieves do not break in and steal. For where your treasure is, there also your heart will be."[3]

"The good man, out of his good treasure, sends out good things; whereas a wicked man, out of his wicked storage, sends out wicked things. I tell you that every unprofitable saying that man speaks will render an account concerning it on Judgement Day."[4]

"The kingdom of the heavens is like a treasure hidden in the field which a man found and then hid. And for the joy he has, he goes and sells all that he has and buys that field."[5]

"Every Teacher of the Law is aware of the kingdom of heaven, and he is like a householder who can, from his treasures, find both new and old things."[6]

"If you want to be perfect, then sell all your belongings and give them to the poor and you will have treasure in heaven and be one of My followers."[7]

3. Matt. 6:19-21
4. Matt. 12:35-36
5. Matt. 13:44
6. Matt. 13:52
7. Matt. 19:21

St. Paul, referring to the treasury in Colossians 2:3, says, "Carefully concealed in man are all the treasures of wisdom and knowledge."

The other tower, the Tower of Babel, is built with selfish motives, by lack of faith, for pleasures, and for escape from the laws of Nature. The building of such a tower is never completed because the builders — ego, vanity, pride, and materialism — destroy the tower before its completion.

The Tower of Babel was built to store earthly treasures. The Lord demonstrated to its builders that no earthly treasury is safe and that no earthly treasure lasts forever because "thieves, rust and moths" destroy it or steal it.

Earthly treasures are, to mention a few: money, precious stones, silver and gold, health, position in society, all other possessions and other perishables. None of these last for long and all are taken away from your hand at the door of death, if not before.

There is another storehouse in the human being; we call it memory. In this storehouse you can find fear, anger, hate, greed, revenge, jealousy, treason, slander, malice, pain, and suffering — images and ideas that are painful and distressing.

People use both storage and treasures. Storage is used to complicate the lives of others and to create hindrances on their path to perfection. Treasures are used to help people, to free, uplift, heal, inspire, and enlighten people. All Great Ones, geniuses, talents, heroes, and real leaders share their treasures as wisdom, knowledge, love, music, poetry, dance, sculpture, and other forms. What a miserable place the world would be if we did not have such treasures!

Look at the world. What would the world be without creative people in the seven major fields of human endeavor, if no one shared with humanity the treasures of the spirit, soul, and mind to build cultures and civilizations?

God in man is the Real Treasure. All other treasures belong to Him, in man. There are higher treasures in man which are the result of age-long labor. For example, healing powers, the power to see the past and the future, the power of higher clairvoyance, the power of higher clairaudience, the power of artistic creativity, the power of renunciation and detachment, the power of serenity, the power of leadership, the power over elements, and the power of continuity of consciousness are just a few.

We are told that the Inner Treasury has nine chambers. One of them contains sixteen treasures, which are

- Love
- Faithfulness
- Serenity
- Joy
- Perseverance
- Self-forgetfulness
- Gratitude
- Humility
- friendliness
- righteousness
- Respectfulness
- Purity
- Creativity
- Generosity
- Knowledge
- Wisdom

One of the greatest treasures is the ability to love. When one says "love," certain people think about sex and about how to use those they "love." Love is the awareness that people around you and all other living beings are treasures. If one treats you like a treasure, his heart will be in you because "wherever your treasure is, there also is your heart."

Faithfulness is a treasure when it is faithfulness to higher principles, great laws, and to the purpose of your life. Do you have a purpose? How can you be faithful if you lack purpose? Faithfulness to goals, to human dignity, to friends — especially faithfulness to human rights and to God in man — are treasures.

One day a girl came to me and said, "I want to marry someone, but he doesn't have any money or a house, land, or other possessions." "But," I said, "he does not smoke, he works very hard, he does not cheat people, he does not engage in malice, treason, or slander. He is loving and faithful. He is so joyful and beautiful." "But," she said, "he has no money." She found herself a very fat millionaire to marry; three months later, she came to me with her eyes all puffy and red from crying. "My life is finished; I am so unhappy...."

In the monastery of my Teacher there was always plenty of food. There were beautiful lakes, flowers, trees, swimming pools, and a stable of healthy horses to ride. He once said to me, "You stay here; I am going to the mountains. Do not come with me." I asked him where he was going. "I am going to live in a cave," he said.

"I will come with you!"

"No," he said. "You are crazy."

"It is better to be crazy and live with you than to be sane and live without you."

He scolded and cursed me to keep me from going with him. But as he traveled, I followed a safe distance behind, hiding in the bushes. Every time he looked back, he saw me trailing behind him like a tail.

"I want only you," I said. "I don't care about pleasures."

I lived with him for three months, serving him like a slave. But in that short time, I saw the glorious wisdom and beauty that radiated from his soul.

Serenity is a very precious treasure. It is a serene mind that reflects great Divine ideas and visions. It is through a serene mind that the power of Spirit flows like a mighty current. It is a serene heart that can dispel all attacks of fear. Serenity is the power to attain victory.

Joy is another great treasure. Do you have joy, or do you get up early in the morning and, with a tomato-red face, begin cursing everything? Do you spread joy to your children, to your spouse, to your friends? When you arrive at the office does everyone hide, or do they come and greet you, hug you, and say, "Good morning"? Sometimes we see terror in the faces of our husbands, wives, and friends. What kind of life is that? Joy is a treasure house. Bring out that treasure and spread it around so that it increases.

The next great treasure is perseverance. Are you spirit, or a jackrabbit — ten steps forward, ten steps back, three steps right, four steps up, five steps left, only to find yourself in the same place? What are you doing with your life?

Perseverance is a steady effort to build your Treasure Tower. What are you doing to build this Tower? M. M. says, "While people were feasting, marrying and enjoying themselves, Noah was building the ark." The flood came and wiped out all the pleasure-seekers. Only Noah and his treasure were safe, because he had the perseverance to build the ark.

The ark is a symbol of his treasure house. He did not just build one side of it and then say, "Let's sleep for ten years." He did not do meditation one day and then forget about it for the rest of the year. He did not read the first page and then forget about the rest of the book. Do not think that because you have a diploma that you are somebody. You are nothing unless you have constructed the treasure house. Your true value is contained in that treasury.

Self-forgetfulness is another treasure. It has taken fifty years of study for me to just begin to understand this treasure. So many speak of self-forgetfulness, but all their endeavor is for their own self-interest. They are just like parasites; our life is parasitic.

Try to be self-forgetful for one day, for one hour, or even for just half an hour. It is something that cannot be explained, but in trying to be self-forgetful you will come to understand what a precious treasure it is.

Gratitude is another great treasure. When you see a person who lacks gratitude, that person is working for evil. Christ said, "One cup of water given to a thirsty man will never be forgotten." The computer of space immediately registers it.

What a great treasure is humility! You see "cabbages" everywhere who claim to know everything. They are everything; they have everything; they can do anything. They are enlightened; they are the Christ! Humility is so simple: it is to know exactly what you are and where you are in comparison to all that exists.

Think about the treasure of friendliness. Are you really a friend? Do you have a real friend? If you "boil" that friendship down, how much reality can you extract?

There were once two friends who loved each other so much that while traveling to the mountains together they made a pact that they would die for one another. One said, "We are one body; we are friends." Suddenly they saw a huge grizzly bear approaching. One of the friends climbed a tree; the other fell to the ground and pretended to be dead. The bear came up to the man, sniffed in his ear, and walked away. The friend in the tree shouted down, "What did the bear say to you?" "Oh," he replied," just that I should never have friends like you who escape danger at the first moment."

Do you have "friends" who disappear at the first sign of crisis? The disciples of Christ behaved this way, especially St. Peter. When he was asked whether he knew Jesus, he replied, "I don't know Him at all; I have never seen Him before." Another person said, "I am sure you were with him." But still he denied the fact. Then a man said, "But I saw you with him." Peter said, "What are you talking about? I don't know Him!" Then he tried to rectify himself by crying. Why do we deny our friends? The history of mankind would have been different if Peter had taken a stand and said, "Yes, I was with Him." But he frustrated the currents of energy; he dispersed them when he said "I don't know Him" to save his own skin.

You cannot have a friend until you become a friend. There is a chapter that is very helpful to read in *Challenge for Discipleship* which talks about being your own best friend.

To be righteous in your thoughts, judgments, words, and manners means to be noble. This is a great treasure.

Respectfulness, to respect God in every living thing is a rare treasure.

Purity in your motives, in your understanding, thinking, and acting is another great treasure.

Creativity is another treasure through which a portion of universal beauty is externalized and shared with humanity.

Generosity is a gem which is the intuitive understanding of the law that states, "Those who give will receive."

Knowledge, as a treasure, is the precious information which tells us how this Universe and all of its parts function as a unit, and how to use that information in relation to life.

Finally, wisdom is a jewel which is the essence, the flower, of our knowledge and experience.

There are other jewels in other chambers of the treasury, such as

- Honesty
- Nobility
- charisma
- Psychic energy
- Gracefulness
- Enthusiasm
- Solemnity
- Sense of responsibility
- Power of leadership
- Power of discrimination
- Simplicity

With these treasures we can make life the most beautiful duration of pleasure and enjoyment; we can create health, happiness, prosperity, and enlightenment.

People often choose their friends or marriage partners by looking at outside appearance and outer treasures.

One must develop eyes that can perceive the Inner Treasures. Without Inner Treasures, all outer treasures become sources of fear, anxiety, pain, and disillusionment.

The current system of mass media spreads news of corruption, failure, violence, horror, death, accident, and murder. Reading the news slowly builds images in our minds that human beings are worthless, that they are a storage of illusion, glamour, and possessions. After building such an image, we lose our self-respect and our respect for others.

This is a satanic attack whose goal is to impress upon the human mind that man is nothing and that no treasures exist in man. This is why regular meditation, performed with deep and sincere gratitude, upon the whole existence as a great treasury, upon Nature as a great treasury, and upon man as a rare jewel in that treasury is so necessary. Often remind yourself how one day your Treasure Tower will emerge from your Core and spread Its blessings everywhere.

Unless we try to conceive and to give birth to that Tower, all other labors performed for peace, right human relations, and unity are useless — because the foundation of these principles is the Treasure Tower.

The Ageless Wisdom tells us that the Chalice, the Treasure Tower within each of us, is built drop by drop by the sweat and labor of the human being. Every time a human being thinks in beauty, acts in beauty, speaks in beauty, lives in beauty, he deposits a jewel into the Treasure Tower. He places a precious stone in the building of the Tower. If you offer beauty to the work, if you do something extraordinarily beautiful, you begin building the Tower. But when you do something obnoxious and ugly, the Tower crumbles. This is the task in which everyone is engaged. From the beginning of life until the present, there is no other labor than the building of the Tower and its unmaking.

If you take a good look at what you are doing, you will see that you are either a builder or a destroyer. Either you are building the Tower within you and within others, or you set out to destroy It with your selfishness, racism, separatism, hatred, malice, and slander. These devils may have value in the marketplace, but they have none within the inner circles. Every time you perform an act of goodness — not with expectation or to show off, but a true act of goodness — you build a section of wall for the Tower. But when you do sneaky, evil, and destructive things, you wipe the Tower out.

Every time you are righteous to your bones in your opinions and judgement, in your work and actions, in your feelings and relationships, you build a pillar for the Tower. When you become unrighteous by stepping beyond your borders, duties, and responsibilities in order to stick your nose into the business of others, you destroy that pillar.

This process continues life after life. Every time you give real joy to others, you increase the treasure of joy. And remember that treasure is something that increases and multiplies to meet your needs whenever you give your treasure to others. With joy, you install a window or another door in the Tower. If in your life you create suffering, worry, anxiety, depression, or hatred in the hearts of other human beings, you destroy whatever you have built in the Treasure Tower.

By making other human beings free, by not imposing yourself, by not making others your slaves, by refusing to exploit or manipulate others, you build the Tower. Have you helped others to think freely, to choose and discriminate freely, to act freely? Have you given freedom to others? Have you helped to free them from their vices, glamors, illusions, vanity, and ego?

Every time you make another human being your slave, or any time you encourage a person to be a slave to their own weakness, you destroy the Tower. You have within you the power to destroy or to build. If you are engaged in destruction, you will be stuck in the classroom of this world forever — suffering, inhaling smog, and being subjected to radioactivity and pesticides. If you are constructive, you will someday graduate from this school we call earth and have a chance to enjoy other creations that God has in this Universe.

There is a story about treasures that helps to give us a different perspective on the subject:

There was once a man who was seeking certain jewels. He was told that he could find them on the top of a very high mountain, so he made all the necessary preparations to scale the mountain and reach the summit. When he was just twenty feet from the top, he fell and rolled all the way to the foot of the mountain and was knocked unconscious.

When he regained consciousness, he saw that he had landed next to a bag of precious stones. He could not believe his eyes until he reached out and touched them. He filled his pockets and returned home.

The Lessons we can learn from this story can be summarized as follows:

1. In certain cases, a person reaches his intended destination only through failure.
2. Sometimes it is in humiliation that treasures of the spirit are found.
3. It is not the desire for treasure that enables you to find it, but the process of suffering that reveals it.
4. Advice often misleads you; the hard facts of life guide you.

2

Dynamics of the Soul

The following illustration depicts the path of the human soul. Let us say that this diagram is the human being:

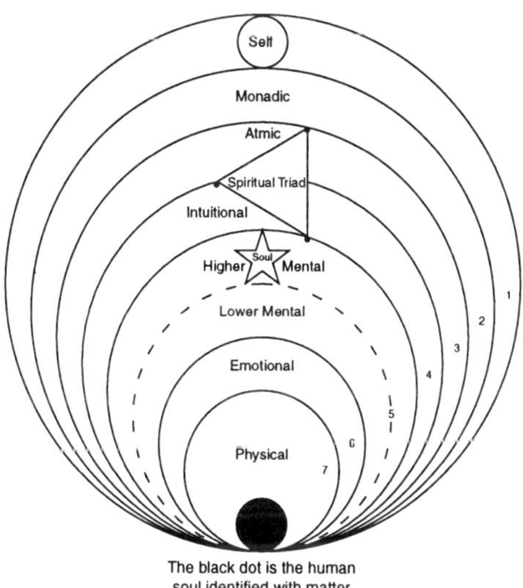

The black dot is the human soul identified with matter

7 — Physical body and nature
6 — Emotional nature
5 — Lower and higher mental nature
4 — Intuitional nature
3 — Atmic nature
2 — Monadic nature
1 — Divine nature

The human soul starts from the lowest level at the beginning and climbs up. The human soul is identified at first with his body. When you ask somebody, "Who are you?" the answer is, "I am this; I am that." That person is identified with his body and with everything that he does at this level to support his body. He is a body-conscious soul but is not yet called a "soul." Millions of people in the world are at this level; they are nothing but bodies.

When the soul progresses, man approaches the level we call emotional consciousness. First he is identified with his physical nature. Then he starts to identify with his emotions. He is now his emotions more than he is his physical body; he is mostly emotional mixed with physical. The person lives in these two levels with all the millions of others who are physical bodies and emotional beings.

When people are in the physical body they are just like cattle and they do not have many problems. But when they enter into the area of emotions, their problems start because on this level they mix with the emotions of others — with family, group, national, and international emotions. All of the problems that are going on in the world are built by emotions.

Often people pretend they are fighting for principles, ideas, visions, and so on, but in reality they are involved with their emotions and they are trying to satisfy their hatred, jealousy, anger, revenge, or fear. It often happens that by involving themselves with negative or positive emotions, they slowly shift their consciousness from the physical to the emotional plane.

If things go well — meaning that the person is going through many emotional troubles — he starts to awaken and think about the cause of his troubles and about the cause of his emotions, and he slowly begins to operate in the lower mental plane. Most of the time our crises, troubles, hindrances, and obstacles force us to awaken and travel from the astral or emotional plane to the lower mental plane to find out the causes of our physical and emotional troubles.

The soul is that which progresses from the physical to the emotional and then from the emotional to the mental plane. While he is in the mental plane — if a person is lucky — he will meet a Teacher, find a Teaching, or find the books, the religion, or philosophy that will tell him that the causes of his physical, emotional, and mental troubles lie within himself. And when he starts to look within, he finds ideas and visions to use for his future development and he progresses to the higher mental plane. When the person succeeds in reaching the higher mind, we say that he or she has become a *soul.*

At Number 7 man is a physical body. At Number 6 he is the emotional body. At number 5 he is the mental body. When these three bodies are really aligned with each other, we say that a man is a *personality*. At this point he has a personality because he is now integrated physically, emotionally, and mentally. Whatever he feels and thinks, he does. His whole nature is integrated and there are no cleavages between his three bodies.

If a person has cleavages, he will want to do something but his mind will say, "Don't do that," and his emotions will say, "It's too difficult or scary." He wishes to do something, but his body says, "I don't want to do this," and his mind says, "You are stupid; don't do it." So he is torn apart. If a person wishes something, he must do it, and he must think, "This is right." If he wishes something, but his mind opposes him and his body objects, he is not unified. Whenever a person is not unified, he is divided within himself. When the cleavages are removed, the person acts as a single unit; whatever he feels, he does — and without conflicting thoughts. When all three bodies cooperate with each other, we say that the man has a personality. The personality is not the outer dressings, mannerisms, or influences. A personality is a powerful human being because all three stations of the soul act together. A strong human being is a person who wishes, does, and thinks along the same line — and because of this he is successful in life.

Success means to be one, to be unified within. If you want to do something but you have doubt in your mind and emotional and physical doubt, you will never be successful because you are not together. When you come together, you are a personality. The most successful people are those who have integrated these three stations of the soul. Sometimes you study, pass your exams, and do everything possible to become successful, but still you fail because you have cleavages in your nature. If you bridge these cleavages and create an integrated personality, you will be successful because success comes when you are unified within yourself.

Psychoanalytical assistance sometimes helps, but if your personality is not integrated, you can be successful for a short while but fail again because cleavages cannot withstand the pressure of success. Christ once said, "If a house is not unified, it cannot stand firm." If your "house" is together, you will be successful.

One can tell on which plane people are by the way they shake hands. They usually shake hands physically or physically-emotionally. If they shake hands in an integrated way, they immediately impress you. When you interview for a job, some people can see immediately whether you are divided within yourself or whether you are integrated. If you are integrated, your looks and manners influence them and give them the impression that you are a unified human being instead of a divided human being. Unity is the dynamic of the soul.

You are going to function as a unit. When you are not a physical unit, you tell your hand to move one way, but it moves in the opposite direction; there is no integration within your nervous system. You want to walk, but one foot moves and the other does not. Again, you are not integrated. If the body is together then you are healthy. If you emotionally love somebody but then in the meantime you hate him, you will say, "There is no success in my love life." Of course there can be no success because you push the gas while in the meantime you step on the brakes! But if your emotions are together, then they are healthy and you will be successful. If your mind is together, the mind is healthy. A man who was opening a business once said to me, "I have invested $30,000 to open this business, but I know that I am going to fail." "Then why are you bothering?" I asked. When the mental, emotional, and physical bodies are together, then the three of them are healthy as a whole and they will contribute to your success.

You are going to be healthy and together physically, emotionally, and mentally. If you wish or desire something, you must do so with all your emotions so that there are no cleavages between your emotions. If you want to go somewhere but you are afraid to do so, then there is a cleavage. If you decide one thing and make a decision that is contradictory to your initial choice, then there is a mental cleavage and the soul does not know which decision to follow. These are the kinds of cleavages that exist within our nature. If we overcome these cleavages, we become a personality.

You cannot become a soul until you become a personality. People think that they are souls, but they are not. They are, in general, their physical urges and drives, their emotions, and their thoughts.

Certain people that you meet may not seem to be striving toward any spiritual attainment with their soul, yet the three levels appear to be coordinated and therefore they fit the rule of being successful. *Spirituality, if defined properly, means progress.* Progressive development, success, and expansion are spiritual because the physical body is spiritual, the emotional body is spiritual, and the mental body is spiritual. You do not need to be religious to be successful. If you are integrated within the three bodies, you can be a holy man — or a monster. If these three are united for selfish reasons, you are a monster; if they are united for a holy purpose, you are a saint.

When you pass from the lower mental plane into the higher mental plane, you advance and start to live in the light of your Guardian Angel — you become a *soul.* A soul is very powerful. When you become a soul, you are powerful because the soul is immediately under the influence of the Guardian Angel who supports the human soul as a mother supports her child. The Guardian Angel is not the soul. The real human soul is you. The Guardian Angel is helping your progress, your development toward perfection. At this level, your motivation changes; and when your motivation changes, you become a more successful person.

Let us say that you have become very successful in your company because you are a personality. Then suddenly you awaken into soul values, into divine values, and your mind expands. Now you begin to use all your income for the development of spiritual values. Your direction changes when you enter into the higher mind. Before this level, you can be successful in everything you do. You can even be a successful thief or a very successful gangster. But when you enter into the higher mental plane, you will slowly change your direction and find the right way to grow in harmony with divine ideas, principles, and purpose.

A thief or a gangster may not be looking for spiritual progress, but when a crisis happens in his life, his consciousness may begin to grow. For example, the girlfriend of such a man may die. He says, "Where is love now?" and so he begins to search through books, or he looks for a teacher. Some say she is in heaven; others tell him about hell. Suddenly something cracks and he begins to understand that all his success was in vain because it did not help him keep the one he loved. He goes through a crisis. I have seen many people turn to a spiritual path when they lose their beloved ones.

Thinking only of money, cheating people, exploiting people, and manipulating people does not work. So when a person enters into a crisis or into difficulties and problems, he creates a certain pressure within. This pressure eventually explodes and destroys the walls in which he encased himself.

We find an example of this in the *New Testament* (Acts 26) story of Paul, who went to Jerusalem to obtain permission from the high priest to kill Christians. Permission was granted, and while on his way to Damascus to carry out his intent, Christ appeared to him and said, "What are you doing?" Paul was so shocked that he totally changed and entered Damascus preaching about Christ. These sorts of things happen to change our direction from materialistic and crystallized living into open, universal, and sublimated thinking. When this happens, we change direction.

We can change in other ways, for example, through dreams. A fifty-four-year-old millionaire who came to the meetings would always respond, "Business is no good," whenever we needed a few hundred dollars to repair the windows or paint the walls of the center. He had seven million dollars in the bank, but business was "no good." One day I said to him, "You know, you could live seven lives with that seven million dollars. Why are you afraid to help people?" He replied, "I must keep what I have because money is very important." Months later he came to my office horrified. "Somebody came in my dream and killed me. I was dead and they buried me. I am terrified. Do you think I am going to die?" "Of course you are going to die," I said, "but I cannot tell you when. You need to come to your senses; one day you are going to die." It took another year before he suddenly became a spiritual man who started giving money right and left to the cancer society, to hospitals, and to schools.

What is change? Change is progress from the lower mental plane to the higher mental plane. A man who changes becomes a *traveler*. Some brotherhoods refer to their members as "fellow travelers." They are traveling from the lower mental plane to the higher mental plane to be a soul.

In the following diagram we see a triangle formed that extends from the Mental Permanent Atom found on the highest level of the mental plane to the Intuitional and Atmic Permanent Atoms. This configuration is referred to as the *Spiritual Triad*. When your awareness focuses in the Spiritual Triad, you are truly a Soul, emancipated from the lower planes. And when your awareness penetrates into the Monadic and the Divine Planes, you are a *Self*.

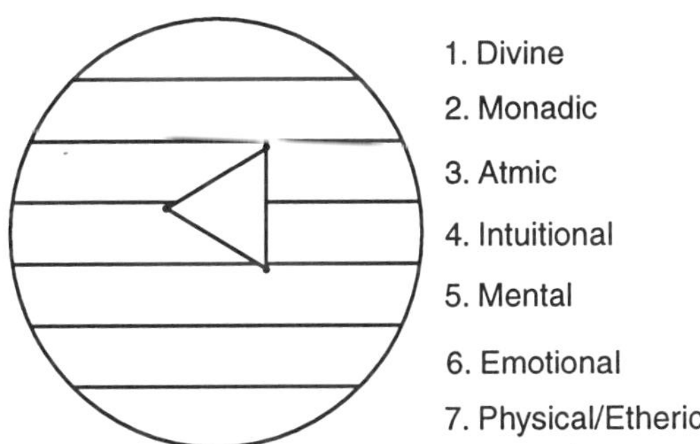

What does it mean to be a Spiritual Triad? Such a person has a very powerful light, a very powerful love, and a very powerful divine will. His will is given to God. He no longer has individual will because his will is God's Will. At the next stage the person becomes the Self. "Self" means that a person has become a Beloved Son, from the Christian point of view, or a Buddha, from the Buddhist point of view.

People advance through crises. Master D.K. said something very interesting: "If you do not have crises in your life, then create a crisis." Discipline is actually a process of creating crises for yourself. You say, "For seven days I am not going to eat." This is discipline, but it is also a crisis. Then you say, "I am never going to drink alcohol again." This is a crisis for your habit. Your habit will say, "You are killing me; give me the bottle." You go through the discipline, but you also go through a crisis. If you do not create crises in your life, Life will create crises for you. Life is God. We live and move and have our being in Him. Christ said, "I am Life." And if you are Life, you are living in Life and Life will take care of you because Life wants to progress. If you do not want to progress, Life will kick you and create crises for you so that you move on.

When you take care of yourself, it means that you are a conscious human being. When you are a conscious human being, Life does not kick you. Life kicks only when you are not conscious and when you are not making spiritual progress. When Christ said, "Be perfect as your Father in heaven is perfect," He meant that we must go forward, progressively onward, and never stop on the path of development and unfoldment toward perfection.

If you do not do this for yourself, Life will kick you. If the incense says, "I don't want to give my fragrance," you burn it and it starts to give fragrance, whether it likes it or not. When you become a soul, you cooperate with God, with Life as a whole.

When I say the word "God," I am not referring to a man sitting around with a beard but to a Great Creative

Power in all the Universe. You can cooperate with this Power and progress from stage to stage, making a breakthrough into higher dimensions.

The Great Pyramid is symbolic of this progression. There is a succession from the lowest level to the King's Chamber, and then from the King's Chamber you can see the Sun, Sirius, and the Pole Star. The Pole Star symbolizes yourself. Sirius represents the Solar Angel. We can find symbols of this progression in every religion and tradition if we open our eyes and look at them without becoming a fanatic in any one branch.

Seven Dynamics

On the higher mental plane, you are a soul; you know your value. When you are a soul, you have seven dynamics, energies, or forces that move things. What does the term "dynamics" mean? Dynamics is a force that moves things, or it is the moving forces in any field.

The first dynamic of the soul is direction. We say that a man has direction when all that he thinks, speaks, and does is for survival, for Beauty, Goodness, Righteousness, Joy, Freedom, Sacrificial Service, and Striving. If he is not doing these things, he does not have direction.

Subjectively, to have direction means to be sensitive to the Will of God. If you are sensitive to God's Will, you have direction. If you are insensitive, you do not have direction and you do all sorts of destructive things in life and do many things without having a direction.

Having direction means that you have a goal in your life — a progressive goal. Direction means that you are concentrated and focused in life. In your thoughts, actions, and speech, you go toward the goal, toward that direction.

You can immediately spot a man who has direction. He is a leader. Eventually he is surrounded by fifty people. You know him. He says, "Let us walk this way and reach that mountain, and then descend the mountain to a spring." He knows the direction. To lead means to have direction. People who do not have direction do not know where to go, and they are confused. They do not have objectives or goals to follow.

Whenever you have real direction, you will sense the oppositions. The moment your soul registers direction, you will immediately find obstacles and hindrances against you.

A twenty-one-year-old girl once came to me and said, "I want to be a disciple." I said, "Wonderful," and sat down with her to lay out a plan for her study, meditation, and exercise. She loved it. I asked her to report to me every month so that I could stay in touch with her progress. Three months passed without a word, when she finally appeared.

"I am sick," she said. "I ache all over." "What did you do?" I asked. "Well," she said, "the discipline was too much and my boyfriend wanted to be with me day and night." Discipleship is not easy. If you want to be a soul, you must sacrifice certain things.

Scientists have discovered that certain fish have a little deposit of magnetically-sensitive metal in their brains that helps them find their direction in the ocean currents. It has also been found in the brain of certain birds; they migrate through waves of magnetic polarity. Man once had this, but he lost it. Humanity no longer has any direction. Their direction is to kill each other: "My nation, your nation, my property, your property, my religion, your religion."

Do you have direction? If you have no direction, you are lost. We lost our direction because we numbed it; it is dead. When you become a soul, the sense of direction in your brain begins to regenerate itself, to awaken and organize itself. From that moment on you have direction. Your words have direction; your life has direction; your relationships have direction.

A young man came to me, saying, "I don't know what to do. I have twelve girlfriends and they are killing me. Every one of them is falling in love with me and I don't know what to do. I love all of them." He had no direction; he was confused. And God save them if any one of them gets a sickness and shares it with all the rest. There is no direction. If we had direction, we would not have so many diseases.

Many obstacles present themselves when we want to have direction. The first obstacle is called inertia. Your body says, "I want to sleep; I am tired. I want to eat and fool around." Because your body has many habits from the past, these habits immediately surface when you try to become a soul. This is why when we begin meditation and decide to become a good person, everything bad happens in our life. From every corner habits arise to prevent our progress because we have spent many, many years planting their seeds in our physical nature and cultivating habits. These habits surface and try to prevent spiritual progress because they think that progress is detrimental to them. These are the physical obstacles that present themselves when we develop direction.

Inertia is harder to overcome for certain people. Sometimes emotions are more difficult to control than the body. If the body is well-fed and taken care of, the body will never create obstacles. But the emotions will. For example, your body wants to get up early and run, but your emotions say, "Let's stay in bed and have a little daydream about your boyfriend," and the body obeys. You start dreaming about sex, and the poor body has all of this dumped on it. Your body was ready to get up and exercise, but your wrong emotions, daydreaming, and desires made it stay in bed. The problems are in the lower mind, the emotions, or in the emotional body. Wherever the problem is, find it and correct it. This is self discipline. People think that by doing a few simple things they can become angels. To become an angel is very difficult. It means lots of labor and sacrifice. By your own work you reach this goal.

Willpower does not help when dealing with habits. You need to analyze the situation. First of all you need to know what the problem is because maybe you are trying to hit the wrong nail. Know what it is, analyze it, and shed the light of your soul on it. When you expand your consciousness and grow, you start ridding yourself of all your "teddy bears." No one told you not to carry your teddy bear to school; you suddenly discover that your teddy bear cannot go to school. Then when you are eighty years old and somebody gives you a teddy bear, you give it away because it does not work for you anymore. When you were a child, it was beautiful. Now that you are grown, it is a deception.

The second obstacle is fear. Fear is the result of identification with old values. Whenever you are identified with old values, you are afraid that you will lose your value, your body, your jewels, your house, your property, your money, your prestige, your name, and your position. Because you are identified, you have fear. But when you have direction, these old identifications and values must be sacrificed to take you to higher values. Unless you sacrifice the old values, you cannot reach higher values because the old values limit your progress and impose themselves on you so that you live within them. If you have direction, or progressive development to advance toward perfection, these old values try to hold you back. You need to sacrifice them. Seeing the old values and the new values, you are between two shores in the ocean and you are afraid to open your sails and travel.

Wrong and confused thought is the third obstacle. We have mixed and confused thinking. For example, your father says one thing, your mother says another, your teachers have their opinions, your preacher his own thoughts, and your friends have different ideas. But something within you thinks that none of them is right. You have the answer, but because all these "flies" are buzzing around in your head, you cannot determine what is right and what is wrong. This is why if you follow the advice of others too often, you never reach your goal because each person's advice leads you in a different direction. You need to overcome this obstacle, which is confused thinking due to immature thoughts, thoughts that are half-built, half-real, half-cracked. You do not need these kinds of thoughts in your mind. Your thoughts must be clear; they must be the bearers of fact and truth so that you do not have obstacles in your mind.

Wrong thought is when one person does or says something with good motives and the other person translates it with his own illusions and glamors and makes it something monstrous. For example, a man's wife is ten minutes late and he starts getting hysterical. "I know where she is," he thinks. "Already she is kissing that man," and by the time she arrives, he is ready to kill her. It turns out that she had a flat tire, and that was why she was late. But her husband had millions of wrong thoughts in that ten-minute period. Another example is when somebody passes you by without saying "Good morning," and you think he still hates you because two years ago you insulted him. It turns out that he did not see you, but in one minute you have fabricated three hundred wrong thoughts.

Another obstacle is ego. Ego is built by everything that we do for our own sake, for the sake of our own interest. People do not like to do things unless there is an interest in it for them. Millions of people live like this. They are strong personalities; they are great scientists; or they exploit, manipulate, and make people work for them day and night. Their egos puff up. They become billionaires with great power, but they live the most miserable lives because they are working only for their egos.

To have direction means to leave your ego and follow God, to follow the interest of the greatest number of people. If you have self-interest, this is good. But if you are also interested in the well-being of your family, you must resign your self-interest and fuse your interest with the best interest of your family. Then you must fuse your family interest with the national interest. Any time you stop, you miss the boat. You need to sacrifice the national interest for the interest of all humanity, for Nature, for all the birds and trees, and for the planet. To have direction means to resign from those limitations that prevent you from expanding toward perfection, toward inclusiveness. This is a very difficult lesson for people; they cannot seem to resign from their selfhood.

Direction is being sensitive to the Will of God. But how do we know if it is the Will of God? Anything that is beautiful, that is good, or righteous, anything that is joyful, and anything that is related to freedom is God's Will. If you make a person a slave, you are not following God's Will. You must try to make the person free. If you make people miserable and sorrowful, you are not in the Will of God. But if you make others joyful, you are following the Will of God.

In all the spiritual scriptures of the world, the word "righteousness" is a key word. If you are righteous in your thinking, speech, judgments, and evaluations, you are a friend of God. You are following His Will because God is righteous. One of the names of God is Righteousness. One of His names is Joy. One of His names is Freedom. One of His names is Goodness; God is Good.[1] When somebody said to Jesus, "You are so good," He replied, "There is only one Good — not me, but God." What He said was so powerful, but people did not understand it.

If you are beautiful in your thoughts, mannerisms, and actions, you are in the Will of God. Every religion gives us information about the Will of God, if we study it. Every re-

1. See *One Hundred Names of God* by the Author.

ligion gives us good advice. The five-pointed star of the coming age is Beauty, Goodness, Righteousness, Joy, and Freedom — God's Will.

If you are identified with your physical body, stomach, sex, or possessions, you will never know God's Will. If your sex says, "Do this!" you think it is will; but it is the will of your sex, not God. You have the wills of your stomach and anger, the wills of revenge, hatred, jealousy, and greed. These are not God's Will. Then you come up with fabrications and deceptions; you deceive people, exploit them, and manipulate them. Only from the level of the higher mental plane do you start feeling what is right and what is wrong. The right things are God's Will. The wrong things are Satan's will.

It is simple. For example, you go to a jewelry store and the shopkeeper is not there, but there is a diamond. If you steal the diamond, you are at one level. If you really wish to take it but you do not, you are at another level. If you want to take it and you steal it very intelligently, you are at another level. Immediately you will know in your heart that you are doing something wrong. Whenever you know you are doing something wrong, it is against the Will of God.

A person knows he is doing wrong, but because his soul is a slave at this level, he does wrong. This is called personality. Personality is either a slave to something good or to something bad. When a person is a unified human being as a personality and you tell him, "Every morning at 5:00 you must be in church," he says, "Yes, sir; of course." He is a slave. It is good to go, but still he is a slave because he is not an independent human being. Then somebody else says, "Everybody must come to the office so we can train you to steal." He shows up because he is disciplined — but he is still a slave to a will that has wrong direction.

The second dynamic of the soul is magnetism. If you do not have magnetism, you do not have the power of attraction. Magnetism is when you attract the right people, the right emotions, the right ideas, thoughts, and visions. You are now magnetic. Your mind becomes so magnetic that the highest ideas are attracted. Sometimes you think that your thoughts are just a vacuum or are non-existent things, but thoughts are electro-chemical substances. When your mind is a strong magnet, you attract different thoughts and synthesize them into something workable.

If you prepare your lessons, lectures, and theses, you become magnetic. You become especially magnetic to your Guardian Angel's suggestions. You also become magnetic to the angels. If you talk about angels, people in society laugh at you and say, "What angels? Where are they? We never saw any of them." But angels are found in every religion, every tradition. Every Great One knows about angels. It is said that Christ commanded thirty-three battalions of angels. It is important to become magnetic to the angels because they heal, make you beautiful, give you courage, give you aspiration and striving, protect you, lead you, and bring the right conditions to your life for you to progress. They are your messengers and your friends.

If you become obnoxious in your thinking, feeling, and activities, however, they will flee from you because you smell very bad to them. Any corruption in your psychology smells rotten. You are going to become aromatic, fragrant. Fragrance is the result of integrity. The chemical composition of elements in conflict creates a bad odor. Chemical compounds in agreement, in harmony with each other, are fragrant. If a group is integrated, there is a group fragrance. If there is conflict within the group, the group has a bad odor. If a nation is together, it is a fragrant nation. If nations fight against other nations, if religions fight against each other, if so-called spiritual people are fighting against each other, there is a very bad odor. Christ said, "Each of you must be fragrant flowers." This is magnetism.

The third dynamic of the soul is the power to reveal. To reveal means to understand things, to see things as they are. Things become real for you, secrets are opened, hidden things emerge. You understand the meaning and the motive, the goal of a speech, an action, or an event. You have a revealing beam of light in your soul so that if somebody comes to you who is hiding in a sheepskin, you immediately know that he is a wolf. You have the power to remove the mask. If he says "I love you," you see behind the words to what he really means.

The dynamic of the soul is revelation; it reveals the motives and intentions. It reveals where an event will lead us.

The fourth dynamic of the soul is the power to balance. You start balancing your life. For example, if a man is totally dedicated to his business and does not spend any time with his children and wife, there is no balance. His wife will say, "I married this man to see his face, but he spends all his time making money, money, money and I am alone without anyone and the children do not have a father." This man is not balanced. Balance means to make money but also to go and spend time with your wife, to take her to a movie or to dinner and have fun together. It is important to associate with your spouse and with your children.

Balance means to create a balance first in your system, taking care of your physical, emotional, and mental needs. If you eat constantly and then sleep, you have no balance. Establish a balance in your emotions, your heart, and mind so that they are in equilibrium. Then create balance in your family by giving them your time. If a girl escapes from home, seeking enjoyment day and night, forgetting her mother and father who are very poor and sick, she has no balance — even if she thinks she is saved because she is religious. She cannot be saved if she has no balance. Because she forgot her mother and father, there is no balance in her life.

The major cause of divorce is a lack of balance. A man comes home from work and says, "Give me a bottle of whiskey," and he drinks and drinks. His wife waits to talk with him or to be with him, but because there is no balance in his life, they separate and divorce.

You must also have balance in your studies. You must study things that are related to your body. For example, you study about your stomach, about sex, about your body and find out what is right for your body. You can study your emotions, your mind, and your business. Study the spiritual level so that you are balanced between body, emotions, mind, and spirit. A man may not care about spiritual things because he has a good body, a good wife, sound emotions, and a good business. But if you ask him, "What gains a man if he wins the world but loses his soul?" he cannot answer. There is no balance. Also, be balanced in your spiritual aspirations.

Do not sit all day and night meditating while your children are neglected. What kind of spirituality is that?

There is a story that Tagore wrote about a man who left his wife and children to search for God in the mountains. But while he was away, God visited his home and waited for him to return.

To communicate with God means to face and meet your responsibilities. If you are not meeting your responsibilities and you think you are saving your soul, you are really deceiving yourself. There are millions of religious people like this. They say "Hallelujah" and think they are saved.

A girl once came to me and said, "I am going to Europe to preach the Bible." When she came back from her trip, she reported, "We were so successful; we revived everybody!" I asked her, "Did you visit your father and mother?" "To hell with them," she said. "What were you teaching in Europe?" I asked. "If you do not respect your parents, I do not care how spiritual you are because you are escaping from your responsibilities."

The fifth dynamic is the power to actualize. Actualization means to bring into objectification your dreams, visions, goals, and plans. If you really want to be beautiful, then become beautiful. People say, "I am a Fifth Degree Initiate." The minute somebody says this, I know the person is unbalanced. Show me by the examples in your life that you are somebody. If you are somebody, then I will believe that you are somebody. Show me. Prove it to me. Actualize your dreams and show them factually in your personal life. This is actualization.

If you want to build a school, you need to actualize it. You must bring it into actualization, step by step. The foundation, the walls must really be built. The fifth dynamic of the soul does this. If you want to be a holy, beautiful, joyful, and magnetic person, actualize these qualities. Let us see them. Let us watch you in your conversation, in your eating habits, in what you do.

The sixth dynamic is the power to aspire. To aspire means to strive to be something better than you were. Physically, emotionally, mentally, and spiritually you are going to aspire. Aspiration is a very great power of the soul.

The seventh dynamic of the soul is the power to synthesize. You are going to synthesize in your life all the beauty you have met, all the beautiful ideas you have had, all the beautiful visions you have seen. If you synthesize them in your life, Beauty, Goodness, Freedom, Righteousness, and Joy live in your body, in your person. You are now a synthesized human being.

A progressive goal is like seeing something shining on a mountain and then going closer to find out what it is. But as you approach, it becomes something else — it is progressive. Progressiveness is not in the goal but in your clarity of consciousness, in the degree of your understanding and assimilation. If a teenager reads this book and is inspired with a certain vision, that vision becomes a goal to his degree of understanding. A twenty-five-year-old will see it differently. It is a progressive goal because people are drawn to understand it better.

When a person finds his direction, he gets himself in a crisis and then discovers his cleavages. He must receive counseling or go to therapists, psychologists, psychiatrists, or religious teachers to bridge these gaps. There are millions of ways to do this. One good source of help is in the book *The Science of Becoming Oneself.* Many psychiatrists are using this book to heal cleavages. The book *Challenge for Discipleship* is a masterpiece to bridge the cleavages. *The Science of Mediation* and *The Hidden Glory of the Inner Man* were written to help bridge cleavages.

Self analysis is good, if you know how to do it. For example, you want to get up every morning at 5:00 a.m. and do meditation, but your body does not want this. There is a cleavage between what you want and your body. Self analysis is to ask yourself and observe why it is that your body is not awakening, why it lacks energy. Perhaps it is because yesterday you dumped a bottle of whiskey into it, or because you are engaged in excessive sex, or you put some bad microbes and germs into it, or you have bad sleeping habits, or you watched television until three o'clock in the morning and the crimes and violent images you saw are running through your nervous system. Self analysis means to find the reason and correct it in order to bridge the cleavages. You can do the same sort of analysis on your emotions and your mind, but it is not easy. Usually you need somebody to lead you.

When trouble starts in your mental mechanism, it means that you are searching and that you are going to find help. That is why Christ said, "Ask and it will be answered, knock at the door and it will be opened." You are in a desperate condition, a crisis, which is a good sign for future unfoldment. Do not be afraid of crises.

There is no happiness when the soul is trapped in the lower levels because these are the worlds of illusion and glamor — nothing but phantasmagoria and fabrication. We need to understand what the mantram, "Lead us, O Lord, from darkness to light, from the unreal to the real, from death to immortality, from chaos to beauty" means. Once you become a soul, many things can happen to your body, to your emotions and mind, but you do not lose your joy. Joy is not happiness. Happiness is physical, emotional, and mental. Joy is found only on the soul level. When you reach this stage, no matter what happens in the lower levels you are above the clouds in an airplane. You can see the agitation of the sea and wind below, but they do not bother you because you are flying above them.

Urgings, striving, and spiritual aspirations are found on every level, and they also push us to move upward. Every time you start striving at something, you get a message from the Guardian Angel, from your physical and spiritual teachers, or from a Great One like Christ, like your Master. Someone kicks you and says, "Get up and get going." If you take this message seriously and listen, you progress. But if you ignore the message, you lose it. Great Teachers say, "We do not always hint. We may only hint once or twice a year." If you listen, They increase the hints. If you do not listen, They say, "He is still asleep. Let him remain in bed until pain and suffering awaken him."

The less you are identified with your personality, the more you identify with your soul. If you are impersonal, it means that you are not identified with the consciousness of your body, emotions, and lower mind. If you are detached and free from these influences, you have greater freedom to solve the problem. If medical science can find the cause of an illness, it is more likely that it will be able to find a cure. If the cause remains unknown, illness is more difficult to cure. In your psychological system, first try to find the causes of a problem. Sometimes it is difficult to find the cause, but go from the result to the cause until you find the real root of why it is happening.

Sometimes when you find the cause it is a situation over which you think you have no control because of life circumstances. When you discover the cause, you need to equip yourself and prepare yourself to attack the cause in the best way possible. But you first find the cause because until you do so you will not know what you are attacking. Suppose you have an enemy hiding in your house, but you think your enemy is a chair. If you fight against the chair, you are fighting against a false enemy — and the enemy will remain until you find it. When you find it, perhaps it will be a big, strong man, and you see that with your own body you cannot eliminate him. So you prepare yourself by gathering four or five friends to tie him up. But you need to find the enemy first so that you know how to deal with him.

3

Responsibility to the Inner Divinity

Responsibility forms the foundation of the laws of success, happiness, health, and prosperity.

An irresponsible man is a man of failure. An irresponsible man is a most unhappy person. He cannot be successful; he cannot even be healthy. Health depends on a sense of responsibility.

We think these things are abstractions and they do not fit our daily life, but they really do fit. If you are really responsible, you have and feel the sense of responsibility, you can see how the energies circulate in your system. Anytime you are acting irresponsibly you short-circuit your own energy. If you watch yourself, you will know these things. You will not even have to read about this because you can see it and you can experience it.

If I act irresponsibly toward my mother and father, my children, my wife, and my grandma, grandpa, I will not feel happy. Why am I not happy? Because I acted irresponsibly.

You have a responsibility to your nation, to humanity, a responsibility to the planet, to the oceans, to the rivers, to the mountains and the flowers. Responsibility is the path that leads you to health, happiness, prosperity, and success.

Responsibility, generally, was covered in the book *The Sense of Responsibility in Society.*[1] In that book I mostly spoke about how we are responsible for the needs of the people. So when you say, "I am responsible for my children," in common language it means you are going to care for those children and meet their needs — physical, emotional, mental, and spiritual needs. So to be responsible means to meet the needs, the demands, the commands of your relatives, of your friends, of your teachers, of your companions, and co-workers. It is all tied to their needs. And you meet their needs if you are responsible.

Today I am going to add another chapter on this topic.

To be responsible means to respond to the command and the need and the expectations of your Inner Divinity. For example, Christ said something very powerful. He said, "You are the Temple of God and within you dwells the Most High." The Most High dwells in us in this Temple. And 2500 years before Christ, Buddha said, "You are, in your Essence, Buddhas," which means you are in your Essence a Divine Light, unlimited light. So that unlimited Light, that Inner, Most High Divinity that is within us must be responsible, and we must respond to that and understand the demands that come with the recognition of the Inner Divinity that is put on our souls. Do you see that? That recognition is putting some responsibility in you. You say, "My goodness, within me there is a Divine Presence. The Most High, the Great Light, the Universal Cosmic Light dwells in me. What is my responsibility to that Divine Light?" Now this is the first step.

1. *The Sense of Responsibility in Society* is available through the publisher.

The second question is a little more dramatic. "If that Most High dwells in me and I am supposed to respond to the demands, the commands, to the expectations of that Most High that is dwelling in me, what about that Most High living in every creature? How must I respond to that Inner Most High?" That is where starts the world peace, progress, spiritual progress, happiness, Nirvana, joy, freedom. There is no freedom if you accept your own Divinity and do not accept the Divinity existing in others. How to do that in this world of hatred, jealousy, revenge, death, and destruction? How to tell these things to people? How to say that within you and within me the Most High exists?

If the Most High exists within you and within our friends, wives, husbands, children, mother, grandma, grandpa; if I am responsible, if I am responding to the demands, to the expectations, to the commands, wishes, and desires of that Inner Most High, what about my responses to the Divinity that exists within you? I am going to respect you. I am going to respond to the demands of your Divinity. How am I going to do that?

Now this is a great science. If we respond to our inner Divinity, our life will totally change. Physically we will put ourselves in rhythm, in beauty. Our emotions will totally change because that Inner Most High will impose upon us Its own rhythm. Our expansion of consciousness will be fantastic because we will recognize the Infinity existing in us and that Infinity existing in other human beings.

And what will happen? I have already stated that responsibility is the source of health and happiness. Why is that? When you are responding to that innermost beauty within you, you are creating a communication line between the Most High within you and your system. And you are releasing the electrical ties within your body, within your emotions, within your consciousness. Now you are tuned. But if you are lying, if you are cheating, if you are hating, there are cleavages between you and the Most High that is living within you. That is what the death is, the destruction is. A Great Master describing a great Teacher says, "His body was so beautiful. His emotions were really like nectar, like blessings. His mind was just pure because he was always in tune with His own Divinity." That was the power of Christ, the power of Buddha, of Zoroaster, and of Krishna. You name Them. Their power came because of Their fusion with Their own Source.

Remember what Christ once said, "The words I am saying to you are not mine but from my Father." He was one with the Father, the Universal Father, the Cosmic Father that is within us.

Now that is the "responsibility" we are talking about. You are responsible for your children, your boyfriend, your girlfriend, your wife, and your husband. If you are really responsible, you are a great man, a great woman. You are very precious. That is wonderful. But what about if you are responsive? You can see, you can talk, you can communicate with that Divinity that is within you. Then you are mighty powerful. We need such kinds of world leaders, such kinds of teachers, such kinds of friends who recognize our Divinity. You have a boyfriend. He always says, "You are stupid." "You are nothing." "You are trash." All right, he is not recognizing the Divinity. He is insulting the Divinity, slandering the Divinity. And whenever you slander your own Divinity or the Divinity in others, you are short circuiting yourself mentally, emotionally, physically. That is the source of all our pains and sufferings in this world.

Now we know that there is a Most High within us, according to the greatest Teachers, and we must develop responsiveness, responsibility between us.

What are the steps? There are seven steps which I am going to explain to you. This is the practical side. If you want to do it, it is so beautiful.

Steps to Develop Responsibility

1. Every day, for a few minutes, observe your thinking, your speech, your words, your actions, and your feelings to see if they are in tune, in harmony with that Inner Divinity. For example, if you are doing something, check yourself. Is that action in harmony with that Inner Divinity? Ask, "Am I responding to the demands of that Most High within me? Am I feeling the Most High when talking politics, economy, everything? What am I saying? Is it in harmony with the Divinity within me and in others? Or is it total chaos? Am I talking about things I don't know?"

So the first thing is to watch and observe yourself. "What am I saying? Are the expressions of my mind, my manners, my will, my actions in harmony with that Most High that exists within me?" That is why a disciple of Buddha, Annanda, said, "Buddha, my Lord, what is the way when living as a friend of Buddha?" "My dear," He replied, "to live as a friend of Buddha means to live in His presence, to think in His presence, to feel in His presence, and to walk in His presence." Wow! In His presence. Can you coordinate your daily life with that Most High that is within you? You can call it any name. It does not matter. We are presenting this as a universal concept, not as a concept of a specific church or a belief.

2. Make people realize that in them exists the Most High. This is so important especially when you are talking in their absence. How to talk, what to talk, what to do, what to write so that always your expressions are in tune with that Most High within you?

There are three techniques that you can exercise without forcing others, without imposing your will upon others. That is another dark side of the human character — forcing and imposing, manipulating, exploiting people, and making them work for your own advantage. That is another dark side of the human being that is so dirty and full of microbes and germs that we must get rid of.

There are three steps. The first is to challenge people: "Look, I was smoking, now I must not smoke. Look, I was so stupid; look how beautiful I am. Look, I was always sad and always criticizing, slandering people, committing treason, etc.; now I am not. Look how beautiful I am now. Look, I couldn't even play the piano and now I am playing the piano and singing. I couldn't even sing with my family; now I am singing in a music center." Challenge them by your example. That is the way you can challenge the Inner Divinity if — that big, big, IF — if you have responsiveness to your Inner Divinity. What are you going to tell them if you are a trash?

Inspire people. You see, there is no imposition. Inspire. Say, "My Lord, bring your peace and understanding to the whole world." Wow, you are inspiring. You are singing, you are playing music, you are dancing, you are painting, inspiring people so that their inner beauty, that Most High that is living within them comes to the surface. You are bringing to the surface their Divinity because you have Divinity within you.

The next step is creating conditions in which they can bloom. Create conditions. You have a child who is a talent. "Mommy." "What?" "Can I have a piano?" "No, what is a piano for you? You don't need a piano. What you need is to make money. Go out. Learn something. Make money so that you can show other people how you can make money." Instead, create conditions for them. Bring a piano. Create great music. Let your child grow. Create conditions. How can you make these plants grow? You fertilize them. You bring them into the sunshine. You protect them. Why is that? These are the right conditions.

Three things you can do. You can condition, inspire, and challenge everybody around you if you have that inner Buddha consciousness, Christ consciousness, Divine consciousness.

We are not advertising Buddhism, Christianity, this or that. We are not talking about the language. Who cares what you are? But if you know that the Most High exists within you, that is the principle. The Most High exists.

Be an example to others. I remember very sadly when one day I was sitting in my office and a mother came and said, "Torkom, this is my daughter. She is thirteen years old and she is a supreme liar. She lies and lies. Can you help her?" "You know," I said, "I am not a magician, but I will try." So I took the girl in and just as I was going to start, the mother knocked on the door. She came in and said, "Martha, don't tell your father that I brought you here." "Mother, what will I say?" "Tell him I was in the supermarket with you." "Lady," I said, "come in, come in. Take your daughter and go. You are the teacher of lying." What can I do?

This is the condition we are in. We do every kind of crime and make other people responsible for our crimes. We must be out of this crime and doing something beautiful for others. Be an example. Your daughter, your children will see that mother was like this, father was like this. What a great memory for them. What a great inspiration for them. One day they will become like mommy, like daddy, like friends, like uncles, like aunts, grandma, grandpa. Until today I have my vision. My grandma was so beautiful. If some difficulty comes, grandma comes to my mind and will say, "That will also pass, my dear. Don't worry. Come, let us go outside and look to the stars." "Yea, Grandma." "Look, look, how beautiful they are. Look how you are dealing with these small problems. Deal with the stars." She is challenging. She is inspiring me. She is creating mental conditions within me to find the greatest existence within my own heart. That is responsibility.

Your prime responsibility is to be faithful to your own Divinity and not let anybody humiliate you because you are the Most High. If anybody is humiliating you, in any manner, this is a crime that he is committing against your own Divinity.

3. The third step in developing responsibility is not slandering any human being who is dedicated to the mission of revealing the Divinity in others. I remember when I went to the library in the monastery and found a book about Buddha. Because that monastery was purely Christian, I put it under my shirt before coming out. Unfortunately the priest saw it and asked, "What is that bulge over your belly?" I said that I ate too much. "Come here. Come here." He got the book out. I was desperate. He said, "Once more if you read these kinds of books, you will be Satan. That man," he said, "is an atheist, against human progress." I said, "So what." Why is he slandering Buddha? Why is he slandering Christ? Why is he slandering Krishna, Mohammet, Moses. None of them must be slandered because they are serving the Most High. They were great Teachers.

You cannot recognize and affirm your own greatness until you can prove that you can affirm and recognize the greatness in other people. You want it more simple than this?

The worst situation in our world is that everybody is engaged in the most miserable work. What is it? It is to slander you, to belittle you, to tell you that you are nothing. That is so miserable. Go to any movie and you can see what they are doing — killing, butchering, and destroying people. Why is that? Affirm the inner beauty and the greatness of human beings. You cannot do that. Why? Because you, yourself, are a phantom of yourself. You hate yourself. You think you are nothing. You think you are fat. You think you will die and you are finished. Someone must raise you and bring you to your senses and say, "You are responsible to the Most High within you." That changes the whole thing.

When you go home, try this. If you have that inner conviction that the Most High is in you, nobody can defeat you. Nobody.

One day a man came and said, "You are stupid, Torkom. You believe in Christ. Christ never existed." I said, "You are lying. He exists." "Can you give a proof to me that Christ existed?" "Oh yes." I said, "Twelve of His closest friends were crucified, beaten and stoned, or butchered for something that does not exist?" He said, "That is an interesting point." If I do not exist but people are butchering my friends, why are they being butchered if they do not love me or are not with me or if they are not protecting me? So I do not exist, really? You are dedicated to me. Your dedication, your power, your devotion, your sacrifice will prove that something exists for which you are sacrificing.

The same thing they did to Buddha. His own cousin, Devadatta, wanted to kill Him and he disturbed the followers of Buddha to such a degree that he became like Satan. But Buddha did not say anything hateful. Read the *Buddha Sutra,* the Devadatta chapter, which explains how much treason that man did against Buddha. One day Buddha with five thousand people sitting around Him said, "My great disciples, friends, Devadatta one day will be a Buddha." He did not say he was going to hell and burn forever. I was listening to the radio and the minister said, "You are going to burn until the end of your bones." My goodness. What is that?

Do you mean that Christ enjoys sending us to hell and sits there, smoking His pipe watching us? What kind of teaching is that? Buddha recognized that even his worst enemy, that no matter what, because there is the Most High in him, he is going to be a Buddha.

4. Spread all the information and Teachings to help people come closer to their Inner Divinity. For example, we published *Other Worlds. Other Worlds* is creating turmoil in the minds of the people. Two days ago, two ladies from New York called me. "Torkom, this book is giving us sleepless nights. I read this book three times. It really burns my heart and mind. What is it?" I said, "Read it more." She said, "Okay, send ten copies." This is not an advertisement. This is really what happened. Read that book and see if you can sleep that night. I really mean it because I did not sleep when I wrote it and read it.

What is *Other Worlds*? If you squeeze it like a lemon you will see that *Other Worlds* says that there is infinity within you, the power of which is everlasting and infinite, and you can have it. That is the whole message.

5. The next step is to spread and encourage those meetings, those gatherings, those groups in which the Inner Divinity of man is discussed.

The other day a psychiatrist called me and said to come in and see what he was doing. I said, "All right." Four people are sitting and each one is saying how much his wife hated him, how much her husband beats her, how much his children cursed him. I asked, "Doctor, what is this? You brought me to hell. I know all these things. Is there anything new?"

"What do you mean?" he asked. "What are you going to do?" "Okay, you sit there and watch what I will do." I said, "Close your eyes." They closed their eyes. I said, "Imagine the most joyful event in your life." Ten minutes later everyone was smiling. Their color changed. I turned to the doctor to see what he was thinking. He had disappeared. He did not stay. After everything was finished, everybody was hugging each other, laughing with each other. The doctor asked, "What did you do to them? Did you hypnotize them?" "No, I made them understand that there is sadness, but man, himself, in his essence, is joy." Bring that joy out because God is joy. God is not weeping and crying, cursing, lamentations, and misery. God is not misery. The Most High is a joyful life, the bliss.

6. **Talk about and spread right things.** Broadcast about Beauty, Goodness, Righteousness, Joy, Freedom, Striving, Sacrificial Service. Do it and you will see what will happen. One day a woman came and said to her child, "Come, come, I am going to visit my boyfriend. You sit here quiet like a mouse." What are you teaching? Teach your boy Beauty, Goodness, Righteousness, Joy, Freedom, Striving, Sacrificial Service, gratitude, blessings. Teach these things because if you teach these things, you will save money. Your boy will grow up and not be a headache for you. He will behave. Most of the husbands and wives say to me, "I don't want children. They are such headaches." Of course, they are headaches if you did not put their heads together correctly.

7. **Expand your own consciousness and the consciousness of those who are related to you and your friends.** Develop in them the sense of responsibility. A responsible man or woman develops courage, daring, fearlessness, detach-

ment, freedom, joy, and service. And it brings you happiness, health, prosperity, and enlightenment.

Think about responsibility.

The real essence of responsibility is the ability to respond to your own Divinity, to respond to the plan and purpose of the captain sitting within you — which is one with the whole Universe. When we say the Most High, it is not me or you. It is in all of us, one.

Q&A

Question: How can we bring out the Divinity in others?

Answer: You cannot really. You are going to bring out your own Inner Divinity first. Then inspire, encourage, and challenge others. Before you are a great artist, you cannot teach anything creative to others. That is why I see many people who are teaching, who have classes, this or that, but what are they teaching? Nonsense! They do not know what they should know. You have to *be* somebody to make a person somebody. The first action comes for yourself. You must feel responsible to the Inner Divinity that exists within you.

For example, let us say that my Father is a King, and here I am in a nightclub, smoking, and doping. Suddenly I see that somebody recognizes me. I feel so miserable — not for me necessarily, but for my Father who is the King. Now do you have this sense that you must not humiliate your Father that is within you, the Most High? That is the source of all responsibility and laws. All moral laws, ethical laws come from the recognition that there is Divinity in me and I must not slander my own Divinity by living a life of cabbages, monkeys, or donkeys. Why would I not be ashamed when I am humiliating my Father, my Greatness, the law, the understanding that is within myself? It is very profound.

Question: In a pragmatic way, how does one get in touch with one's Divinity?

Answer: They are the seven ways that I gave you. The first thing is this: try to recognize in every man that there is a Most High in him. And then try to make your thoughts, your words, your actions in harmony with the understanding that you have about that Divinity within you.

For example, you say, "You know, really that beauty exists in my essence. Here, here is the beauty." Okay but then you start doing otherwise. And you say, "Yea, I talk about my being a beauty, but look at what I am doing." Okay, if you change that, you have the first connection with your beauty. It is a work you are going to do for yourself. Nobody can help you. People say that if you come to our church, if you listen to these sermons and these lectures, you will be in the "seventh heaven." This is the most ugly lie. Nobody can take you to heaven. Nobody can lead you to heaven or paradise. It is you with your own striving and efforts who must gain the merit to be in that state of consciousness.

Question: *How are we supposed to know what to do, to think, and to feel about what is going on in the world, about what we hear on the news?*

Answer: Well, if you cultivate your own Divinity, you will not depend on news because your Divinity will let you feel exactly what is going on. When you feel what is going on, that Inner Divinity will tell you what to do.

For example, yesterday a woman called me and said, "Torkom, you told us to say seven times the Great Invocation and it will help the situation. It is not helping." I said, "Continue. Do not give up. Just send telegrams to God and say, 'You know what is happening here. If it is what you want, it is all right, but if it is not what you want, stop it.' " There is no faith. Bring your faith out. I did not give up. I am not going to give up. Everything is going to be nice according to His will. I am not afraid. Do not worry about it.

Question: *When I think about responsibility, I think about Gandhi. Can you explain?*

Answer: Oh yes. Let me tell you one thing about Gandhi. Gandhi was a very powerful man. He could mobilize six hundred million people and attack the British Army. But he felt responsible to his own people and to the British people. They said, "Gandhi, you are a very dangerous man. We are going to put you into prison." He said, "All right." They put him in prison and they asked him, "What do you want to read?" He said, "Bring me the *Bhagavad Gita.*" He translated the *Bhagavad Gita* in the prison, and when he became victorious, he said, "I learned all the techniques and tactics to overcome the British Empire from the book, the *Bhagavad Gita.*" What is the Bhagavad Gita? The *Bhagavad Gita*'s main purpose is to say that there is a Divinity in you that cannot be conquered. Gandhi said that if it is true, then he was going to be a conqueror. And he did it. That is a great man.

Question: How do you act responsibly when other people act obnoxiously?

Answer: When you think that somebody is obnoxious, it means you are superior and he is obnoxious. This duality conditions your thinking and behavior about how obnoxious that man is. You are controlled not by your inner Divinity but by the obnoxiousness of that man. That obnoxious person is controlling all your behavior and you do not know it. So the first thing is to recognize your Divinity. Tell your "enemy" to recognize the beauty of your enemy. Can you?

Question: I am trying.

Answer: No, you are not trying. If you really recognize within yourself that he has Divinity, you will find ways and means to change that person. You do not think I have enemies? My goodness, for thirty years I have been standing here. There are enemies like mushrooms coming from every place. How am I living? That is the technique. Mushrooms. You turn left and they hit from your back. You turn right. They hit in the chest. You will conquer by beauty.

What does Nicholas Roerich say? "We pray with beauty. Through beauty We conquer." Your enemies will go and die and perish, but your beauty will remain forever.

Question: *Sometimes responsibilities conflict with one another. Is their any hierarchy of responsibilities?*

Answer: Of course, but to respond I will not believe that responsibilities are competing. When you have responsibilities and you cannot measure which is the first, which is the second, that is all right. They are the same responsibility or a branch of it, but there is no conflict in the responsibility. If you are really responsible to your inner Divinity, you will see which is the first, which is the second. You will have enough light, enough courage and daring and intuition to take the first thing first and the second thing second. But your first responsibility is to manifest the Most High that is within you with all your thoughts, actions, and words. If you can do this for two hours, I will come and help you tonight. For two hours be really divine, and in those two hours every kind of temptation will come to you. They will bug you, all around you, to demonstrate whether you are really responsible or not responsible.

A woman writes to me and says, "Torkom, immediately I sit in meditation, my children, my dog, my cat do everything possible to take me out of my meditation." I said that they are trying, demonstrating, and showing you where you are. The world is a computer. The whole space is a computer. Life is a computer. Nothing happens without a plan, a cause, and purpose.

***Question:** I watch television to find out what is going on in the world. Is that OK?*

Answer: Even that I do not recommend. My position here is for one thing — always from beginning to end to emphasize that you are really Divine in your Essence. Hold your Divinity, honor it, and feel proud of it. And do not let anybody humiliate your beauty. You will feel that kingship within you. Try to get closer to that Inner Divinity and you will know — without radio and television. You will know what is happening because in the intuitional level there is no reason and logic. There is only information. It is instantaneous understanding and we must try to go there if we really do not want to fail in our incarnation. People are coming here but most people's Divinity has been aborted with trash. Do not be aborted. Be your Inner Divinity and affirm it. Try to demonstrate that you are really beautiful, that you are really something. You are so generous. You are so kind, so compassionate. You are so artistic, so sensitive that you love people. If you have thirty, forty people like this, you will change the world. Your ammunition is not bombs. Your greatest ammunition is ideas, visions. All these other things will pass. See how many great empires have been destroyed. They are like the sands of the earth, but these ideas exist until now.

4

Journey of the Soul

When does the progress of the human soul start? The first step for the spiritual journey is the awakening from long years of sleep. Suddenly you awaken from the life of your body, from your emotional interests, your mental traps in which you slept for many years, maybe many lives without knowing where you were going, what was your destination, what was your purpose. Most of humanity is in that state.

The first sign that you are awakening and starting your journey toward "home" is that you suddenly realize you are missing something very important in your life, but you do not know what it is. Have you had that experience? That is a very important spiritual and psychological moment when the memory of "home" dawns in your heart. You do not know yet what is "home," but you are very uncomfortable in this stage of consciousness and being.

You start questioning and try to find the destiny of your life. Of course, your search passes through many years, many incarnations. You may go to wrong addresses. You may trap yourself many times thinking you are going North but actually you are going South. You take wrong freeways and suddenly you reach a place you never wanted to be. That is the "fun" of spiritual life. But eventually somebody or something tells you that the purpose of your life is in "that" direction. So when you hear these words, your soul, your inner being tells you that it is the right direction — and you say, "Let me follow."

The second point that awakens you is the time when you go through a painful experience, a defeat, a loss. Some crisis hits your life and you awaken. Before that you were sleeping very happily. Life was very beautiful for you, everything was rosy, and your table was full of everything, and you had lots of friends. Suddenly lightning hits you. That is a very fantastic experience. You find out that all the things you were leaning on suddenly disappear. What remains? Your body, emotions, and mind. Suddenly you feel that even your body, emotions, and mind cannot help you. That is the moment you make a great effort to contact the one you must trust. That is your Self, your Higher Self, which is the door of spiritual progress. You go toward your own Core, feeling that the only refuge is in your Core. Individuals, groups, nations, even races often come to such a conclusion.

The third critical time is while you are awakening, you hear the call of your Soul or your Master. He says your name and asks, "How long are you going to wander, how long are you are going to be occupied with your monkey business? Come to your senses. Take your progress in your hands." In that moment, through the voice in that call, you sense your destination. Some of you have had this experience. Some of you are called "from refreshment to labor." You were taking it very easy, but suddenly the voice came and gave your name and said, "That is enough. The time of childhood has passed. Now different duties and responsibilities are going to be put on your shoulders. It is better for you if you prepare yourself for such a responsibility, task, and labor."

The fourth crisis comes in your life when you suddenly realize that you are the architect of your life. It is you who is responsible for whatever you are now. You start searching and discovering the great law of cause and effect. Whatever you sow that is what you are going to reap. Suddenly serenity and joy fill your heart, making you aware that no one else is responsible for what you are now. Only you are responsible. You live in certain ways and now you are reaping the seeds that you have sown in the past. That is a fantastic experience — to take the helm of your life in your hands. You drive your own "car." The car obeys you and you say," From now on I am going to live in a way that in future lives not only will I enjoy the life but also I will do my sacred duty to the Universe and to all kingdoms," because the cause and effect show that you are a part of the great Universe. You start living in such a way that not only do you become happy, beautiful, prosperous, but also you help everyone in the world to be happy, healthy, prosperous. Now you understand that without making other people beautiful you cannot be beautiful; without making other people prosperous you cannot be prosperous. The wholeness of the Universe dawns in your mind.

Once these four steps are taken you are ready to start your journey. The path of your spiritual life is open and you are ready to walk on that path.

The first step after you are awakened is to be in charge of your body. That is how you take the first initiation. You control your body, the vices of the body, the habits of the body, especially sex drives and urges and eating habits. Your body appears to you as your car now. No matter how many books you read, what degrees you have, they are not important, for they do not make you progress on the path. It is not your knowledge, it is not what you read, it is not what you collect that makes you progress on the path. The only thing in this stage that makes you progress on the path is to control the body, so that it is healthy, happy, and harmonious with your destination. Your body eats only whatever you want it to eat, drinks whatever you want it to drink. Never abuse your body because your body is your car and Temple and God is living within you. You are that God in your body. So you are going to watch your body, your sex life, your eating habits. Millions of people are devastated because of their uncontrolled sex, eating habits, and laziness. You are going to control your sex because in the process of sublimation your whole system — your brain, chakras, ganglias, glands — is nourished by sex energy.

Second, you are going to control your habits of eating, drinking, smoking — coffee, coffee, coffee, cigarette, cigarette, cigarette. Can you stop them? A little cigarette controls a big man, a big woman. Alcohol! Some people see a bottle and they die for it! What is inside? Something that destroys your future. You can smoke a little if you want, drink a little if you want, but do not let them control you. Once you are controlled you cannot achieve the first expansion of consciousness. The first expansion of consciousness is entering into the light and developing the ability to control the divine mechanism that is given to you by the Universe. This body is your divine mechanism. For example, you stay up until three or four o'clock in the morning watching television. Most television programs are hallucination, deception, manipulation. Of course, there are good things also. But to be crazy is to sit and watch until two or four o'clock how people are killing each other. What will happen to your consciousness the next day? You are polluting all your system until morning with these crimes and ugly thoughtforms, and what are they doing? They are taking your soul into those caves and corridors where these crimes are committed. You are polluting yourself, polluting your children.

How are you going to approach your body? You are going to approach your body as if it were a divine temple given to you as the greatest gift from the Universe and handle it as the most precious treasure.

One day I was sitting and watching how people walk. They walk like camels, elephants, birds, coyotes, foxes. They do not know how to walk. Today, watch how you are walking.

The body is controlled and dedicated to a great purpose. People say, "I have taken the Fifth Initiation." I say, "You cabbage! How could you take the Fifth Initiation?" They can fool themselves but not you if you are awakened. The first initiation is taken when your body is really under your own control. And your body does not put pressure on you and force you to be its slave. Either you are the owner of the body or the body owns you. If the body owns you, there are many, many dangers.

The greatest danger is to be attached to your body and be a slave of your body, which prevents spiritual energies, higher energies from circulating through your system, and you become earthbound and share earthly karma. You cannot lift yourself up and share divine karma. This is the first initiation. Of course, the Rays are involved, centers and chakras are involved.

The second step on the journey of the spiritual progress of the soul is taken when you start controlling your emotional life. Most of the problems in your home, of husbands, wives, and people around you originate from your body and emotions. When a body is not controlled, the emotions run wild! Those who can control their emotions are masters of life and create such a magnetism that divine energy circulates through them.

To control your emotions there are five vipers you are going to annihilate from your system. One of them is *hatred.* Do you like this color? "I hate it." "I hate my mommy, my daddy, my wife, my husband, my children. I hate my boss." Really? Do you know what you are doing? You are committing suicide. Whoever works against love commits suicide. This is an absolute law. Do not work against love.

You are also going to control *anger*. Do you know that most problems of life are the result of anger? In an angry moment you kill people, you destroy nations, your family, your children. Anger must be eliminated from your life. Instead of anger, understanding must prevail.

The third viper is *fear.* How much do you control your fear? You do not know what fear is. Fear is the termite of the building that is within you. Termites are eating you. Because of fear you feel negative. You act irritable. You attack people. You destroy others because you are afraid.

Not only are human beings caught in these vipers, groups are also caught in them as are nations. Because of fear they do things they would never do if they did not have fear. Fear kills your stomach, your kidneys, your lungs, your throat center. How can you keep your temple healthy, beautiful if you are living in fear?

Fear is a great cause that prevents your contact with Higher Forces. If Higher Forces give inspiration to you, impressions to you, you will use them in the wrong way because of your fear. They do not give treasures to you because you will misuse them through your fear. You are going to find how to overcome fear so that you take the second initiation.

The next one is *jealousy*. Jealousy is an entity living within your aura. If you bring a clairvoyant he will see it and say, "Somebody is eating you within your aura." That is jealousy. People think jealousy is an emotion. It is not! It is a dark entity working for your destruction. It destroys families, groups, and nations. Once it enters, it finds a way like a gopher through one man to another man, one woman to another woman, and eventually it destroys good relationships. That is jealousy.

People think, "I am a second degree initiate." Do you know what it means to take an initiation? It means to work so hard against your own stupidities and limitations that eventually you corner yourself and say, "I am the soul; you are the bodies. I have to achieve great heights." How can you do that? Nobody can help you except when you start actualizing the Teaching, the advice given by your Teachers and Sages. You are going to actualize the Teaching and the advice.

The next one is *revenge*. Revenge is devastating our planetary life despite the Teachings of the Ageless Wisdom which caution us against revenge. Anybody who steps on your tail you say, "I will take revenge." When you take revenge you throw yourself three hundred lives backward in your evolution. That was the message of Christ, "Love each other." Forever! A disciple came and asked, "Can we forgive our friends if they do wrong seven times?" He said, "Seven times seventy is not enough." What He wanted to say was, instead of developing in your mind poisonous snakes of revenge, develop love and forgiveness. That is how angels open the path for you to Higher Worlds. If you have destructive people around you, and you want to bring them to their senses, revenge is a terrible mistake. The best way is diplomatic, educational ways, by which you bring them to their senses.

Your emotional body becomes purified and starts reflecting your intuitional body. The divine impressions and visions gradually become reflected in your life, and you see the beautiful changes in your life. You love, you are pure, and you free yourself from all these materials and elements that are sapping your life, blocking your path and not letting you to go to your destination. Once you understand this you will do everything possible so that nobody and nothing hinders your progress on the Path. That is why you are created. A Greater Master says, "If you want to know where you are going to go, stand outside and look at the stars. Look how many million miles and years you need to reach them." Who are the stars? The stars were once upon a time human beings like you.

Because you have a body, you identify with physical objects and live for them and forget about your destination. Actually, if you want to know, all objects of the senses are collecting a supreme illusion. The Master Tibetan calls them "shadows." They are shadows.

If you have taken the second initiation your third step on the path of spiritual development will be to build your mental body. The mental body is like the temple that you have to build. You collected the material. You cleansed your body and heart. Now you have to build a temple. That temple is in your mind, in your mental body. There is also a Chalice in your higher mind. It has twelve petals.[1] For each initiation a few petals open like a huge rose. When nine of them are opened you become a Third Degree Initiate. Each petal is an electrical energy related to the zodiacal signs, to your centers, to some constellations. You become a temple in which the great mystery and wisdom live and abide.

How are you going to build your temple? There are five things in your mental body that you are going to conquer. The first one is *greed*. Greed is a worm that eats your mental body and stops your progress as if your tail were frozen in a lake and you cannot jump out.

One day a tiger said to a cat, "How do you go and fish and eat from the river?" The cat said, "Well, I will give you the secret. Come to the lake. You see this hole? Put your tail through that hole. Very soon you will feel millions of fish hanging from the hairs of your tail." The tiger said, "Alright." The cat was very much afraid of that tiger. That tiger was eating her children, her uncles, daddy, this or that. The cat

1.See also *The Subconscious Mind and the Chalice.*

said, "I must fix him." So, the tiger sat with his tail in the hole. Soon the hole froze over. Half an hour later, he said, "Wow! I feel lots of fish hanging from my tail. How can I carry all these fish?" So, he tried again and again to pull out his tail, but it was frozen. He said, "I must make a last effort to pull all these fish out." The last effort cost him his tail!

That is what a greedy man does. He hangs his tail in greed into matter and matter gets him. Money, money, money, furniture, furniture, furniture! This possession or that item, and you lose your head and you die. Instead of living ninety years you live sixty years and they dump you into the hole. You made so much money. You were so successful. You were greedy for everything. Stop greed.

How can you conquer greed? By having and using the things that you need. God save you if He comes to your houses and finds five hundred things you never use.

One day I was visiting a friend. She had seventy-one pairs of shoes. I said, "Are you using them?" "No," she said, "I never use them, but I will." "When," I asked. "You are eighty-seven." Still she goes and finds nice shoes and buys them. "When are you going to use these?" "Later." When is later? Life is gone. The seventy dollars you gave for the shoes, give to somebody who needs it now. Build a hospital. Build a school. Build a university. Give your money and make people read books. Help people who do not have bread to eat instead of accumulating things.

The second mental vice is *ego*; you feel big. "Nobody is better than me. How can you insult me? How can you step on my tail?" That is ego. The first sign of ego is you feel hurt when people speak the truth. It is so subtle. When you see somebody is speaking the truth you feel so uncomfortable because the ego fears the truth, especially if it hurts his interests. He thinks he is the only one. What is the essence of it? The ego separates you from God. No one must exist in you except God. If you separate yourself from God Who is everything, in everywhere, you become a tumor in the body of His wholeness. Who cares how many books you have read, or which universities you graduated from? Actually most criminals are university graduates. It is not knowledge we need; we need spiritual actualization.

We asked our Master, "Master, how can somebody be a Master?" "By mastering," He said. Mastering? There should be something to master so that you become a Master. What are you mastering, your ego? Let it dissolve and think every man is as beautiful as I am. Every human being needs to be happy as I want to be happy. Everybody must be humble as I am humble. You cannot separate yourself from that unity of life. The ego prevents you from entering your innermost Temple where God lives. The first conquering is greed, the second is ego.

The third is *vanity*. Vanity must be conquered. Vanity is the assumption that you know more than everybody, you have achieved more than everybody, you can do things better than anybody. These eventually lead you to isolation and misery.

The fourth is *fanaticism* — fanaticism of anything, everything. Fanaticism closes the windows and doors toward life and light, and life and light cannot come in from the Universe. One becomes a slave, a prisoner of ignorance, because of his fanaticism. Because of fanaticism he always imposes his will upon others. He always insists that his religion, tradition, and ideology are the best. This is a hallucination. There are so many beautiful Teachings all over the world. Do not be closed to the values that exist everywhere. You must be a searcher of diamonds. You must look for diamonds. Wherever you find a diamond, take it. Do not say that only this diamond is good and not others. Do not fool yourself.

The fifth one is *separatism*. There is color separatism, sex separatism, national and racial separatism. What has this done to the world in so many centuries? What is it doing now secretly, underground?

Try not to be involved with these emotional and mental monsters and vipers. Some people, when they open their mouths, nothing comes out but ugliness. How can you be a temple of God? The victory over these five monsters makes your consciousness shift from physical, emotional, and mental planes to the higher mental plane, where your consciousness will be focused. Once your consciousness is focused on the higher mind you become serene, you think clearly. You see your path and where it is leading you. You see your visions and slowly your divine faculties, the psychic powers that are hidden within you start unfolding.

Let us take the fourth step. In the Fourth Initiation you decide, "Whatever I am, whatever I know, whatever I can do are all dedicated to humanity. I am a great sacrifice given to humanity to enlighten them, to lead them, to protect them, to sanctify them, and lead them to their destiny."

There are three steps that take you from the mental plane into the next plane. First is clear thinking. In other words — total righteousness. If you are not righteous in your feelings, in your thinking, in your acting, in your decisions, in your plans toward people, toward animals, toward everything, you cannot take the Fourth Initiation.

At the time of Lot, three Great Ones came to the city and said, "We are seeking people who are righteous," because only righteous people will be saved from humanity and be transported to a level that will be safe for them. What is the safest place? The Intuitional Plane. There is no safer place than your Intuitional Plane. It is called sometimes Christ consciousness. You enter into the Christ consciousness. Even your individual consciousness is eliminated. We call that kind of consciousness on the Intuitional Plane, awareness. You are aware without logic, without deduction, without reasoning. You are aware.

In this fourth step, the Fourth Initiation, you become an Arhat. An Arhat is a man Who conquered the body, emotions, mind, and higher mind, and now is ready to go to the Intuitional Plane and dedicate himself to the Plan and Purpose of God.

Look how beautiful the journey is. It takes millions of years, maybe a very short time if you really work hard. It depends on you. If you do not have accidents on the path, if you do not have lots of karma, you can go faster and safer.

One day a man came to the valley and asked a garage man, "I am going to Los Angeles. How many hours will it take?" The garage man was a funny man and answered, "Fifteen minutes or three hours." The visitor said, "Are you out of your mind? Three hours is something, fifteen minutes is something else." "Well sir, that is what I know," said the garage man. So the man drove on the freeway and had an accident. The police came, the fire engines came. At last he reached Los Angeles in four hours. "Now I understand the wisdom of that garage man." So you can go to your destination in a shorter or longer time. It depends on what you are doing. Are you fooling around?

The other day I was giving a lecture. I said, "Some people put their rice on the stove and go and watch television, and when they come back the rice is burned with the pot. You burn your rice and your pot while your body is fooling around, and not standing on its duties and responsibilities. You are going to take your salvation in your hands. You are going to unfold your inner potentials. You yourself know your destiny, where you are going, what to do, how to do it and not depend on others. Depending upon others means you are not cultivating the powers that are within you.

After the fourth step the greatest step comes. The fifth step is called the Hierarchical step, by which you eventually go and enter into the gate of the Hierarchy as a Master and see the universal Plan. You educate yourself in such a way that the mysteries of the planet, creation, constellations, zodiac and galaxies slowly, slowly are revealed to you and you look back and say, "Look, humanity is living like cattle. What can I do for it?" Sometimes you come back as a Christ, as Krishna, as other Great Ones came. They came back. They led humanity from darkness to light, from the unreal to the real, from death to immortality, from chaos to beauty. Planetary forces and energies are in the hands of the Masters. That is also your destiny. You are going toward it. But how many million years will it take? To be able or not depends on our efforts. That is why we must not lose time but be on the alert. Daily meditation. Daily review. Daily discipline. What are you doing daily? What are you not doing? Why are you doing? Are you in the right direction or wrong direction? Check yourself and find out through your meditation and studies and listening to your Teacher so that they put your wheels on the line, leading toward the destination.

The sixth step is called Service for the solar system. Man graduated from the planetary school and is entering now the solar system college. Isn't that beautiful? He decides what to do. At the Sixth Initiation the Seven Paths open. The Masters choose one of them, because at this stage Cosmos is open to Them.

After the Sixth Initiation, the seventh step opens. The Seventh Initiation is service to the Purpose of God. You can see how slowly a trash collector becomes a master mind.

These visions must be given to you so that you move a little. Move forward. The Seventh Degree Initiate finishes the Cosmic Physical Plane and enters into the Cosmic Astral Plane. The Great Ones Who are working for our salvation look at you, examine you, and eventually fit you to the labor that you can do.

We are slowly, slowly learning ABC. Your teacher says if you write a letter, write that letter perfectly because maybe in space you are going to be a reporter. Your computer, instead of having one list, will have ten thousand lists there. Cosmic information and communication systems are within you.

After the Seventh Initiation, the Eighth and Ninth Initiations come. You reached the Temple. What do these stories tell us? All these stories tell us that you have limited time. Do not listen to those philosophers who say time is limitless and you can fool around as long as you want and eventually everything will be alright. Eventually everything will not be alright. You can be eliminated, totally evaporated and annihilated if you do not fulfill the time limit and reach the stage where you should have reached to pass the gate.

Q&A

Question: What is the eighth step?

Answer: The eighth step is called Transition. The ninth step is called Refusal. These are symbolic words.

Question: Would you relate the chakras to the degrees of initiation?

Answer: In the first initiation four etheric chakras must be controlled. They are the base of spine, sacral center, solar plexus, and spleen. These four must be under your control. When you are finishing, the etheric heart center, throat center, and head centers must be unfolded. The petals of the Chalice also must be opened. For example, a second degree initiate must have six petals of his Chalice open. You say you are a Third Degree Initiate. A clairvoyant will look at your petals and say, "You are a cabbage, nothing else." The Tibetan Master, talking about these things, says that in the future advanced schools will be controlled by two clairvoyants who will sit on both sides and when a man or woman is coming to be a member they will check their chakras, and they will say "Yes" or "No." You can fool most everyone except real clairvoyants.

A Third Degree Initiate must have nine petals open. At the Fourth Initiation, the innermost three petals that were enclosing the fire — the divine fire, the spiritual essence of man — open and the fire burns all petals and the temple is destroyed. The human soul is now free.

> ***Question:*** *You were talking about the physical body and its dangers, and one of the dangers was that the energy does not circulate through you and you become earthbound. Can you explain?*

Answer: Disease is an abnormal condition; sicknesses are abnormal conditions; wars are abnormal conditions; even an earthquake is an abnormal condition. All these things happen because of an imbalance of energy circulation. Your body lives with two energies. Your car operates with two kinds of energies. Your battery has one cable positive and one that is negative. Take one of them out and your car will not run. You have spiritual energy and earth energy. These balance each other and your life runs. If you are cut from the spiritual energy you develop sicknesses. What is sickness? Sickness is when the earth is going to eat you. Eventually you die and earth eats you. That is what happens. Eventually you are going to learn. When you are a Fourth Degree Initiate you no longer die. You let your body sleep and you ooze out consciously. You say goodbye to your body.

That is why snakes are the symbols of Initiates. They leave their skins and come out without dying. That is what you are going to do. Leave your body and the skin is left, consciously you come out. This is what you are going to learn.

> ***Question:** You were speaking about the time element that runs out for individuals. Can you explain this?*

Answer: God gave you life. Carry that light, that torch until the end. Do not let any stupid things stop your progress.

A girl, who was a student, wrote that she cannot meditate because her boyfriend was fooling around. I asked her, "Don't you have greater interests than your boyfriend?" Your spiritual progress is of supreme value. You cannot sell your diamond for a stone. How precious you are. Unfortunately, all our television programs, newspapers, and books tell you, "How stupid you are, how nonsense you are, how valueless you are. You do not have value. What are you? Nothing. One bullet can kill you and you are finished." They put this trash in your mind and slowly, slowly you believe that you do not have value. That is why Christ said, "You are Gods." Look at what He is saying. He did not say that you are trash. He said, "You are Gods." When is that God going to manifest itself? How long will it take? Ask yourself every night, "Did I manifest my God today? Or was I really a monkey?" You find yourself and every day try again and again and again.

Do not give up because this is a chance for you. This life is a great chance for you. Save your time. Save your emotions. Save your money. Save everything so that you focus yourself on your spiritual progress. Do not depend on anybody else. Depend on your Inner Lord, and open your ears and eyes and listen, and let your Inner Lord guide you.

> ***Question:*** *You were speaking about controlling the body. Many people who have been doing something over a period of years, such as habits, want to change but they are always reminded of their past. Doesn't that hold them there?*

Answer: There are books. There are teachers. You must discriminate what you are reading, where you are going, to whom you are listening. You will see that the right books, the right teachers do one thing — lead you into Beauty, Goodness, Righteousness, Joy, and Freedom. And later if you assimilate these five you go two steps ahead: spiritual striving and total commitment for the service of the Hierarchy. Total commitment — no matter what. Where are these people? We listen to these things, then go and forget about them. You are going to take action now. Prepare yourself for greater and greater striving and fight against those forces that try to tie you to your lower self.

> ***Question:*** *Do we have a responsibility to take part in the earth's initiation?*

Answer: Of course. When we say humanity, we sometimes think in a certain way. What is humanity? Humanity is one big man. We are cells in it, little, little cells. What are groups? Little chakras. What are nations? They are organs in that human being. Humanity is only healthy when the cells and the chakras and the glands and the organs are healthy and in good cooperation in that body. That is how we can have a happy humanity. Organs are fighting against organs. The leg fights against the hand. The nose fights against the ear. The eyes fight against the teeth. What kind of humanity is this? So think in terms of unity.

Hiawatha and the Great Peace speaks about the future order of humanity. Hiawatha was a great Master. He came to America and His teaching became the foundation of the American and French constitutions. Real democracy came from Hiawatha. If you start reading that book tonight I bet you will be sleepless until morning. You cannot stop until you finish it.

Question: What happens in the world that is not natural according to our molecules, God given molecules and atoms, that are not a part of God?

Answer: If you lie, it is unnatural. If you cheat, it is unnatural. God never told us to lie, to cheat people, to manipulate and exploit them. That is not natural. You asked for one thing. I said four things to you.

Question: How can it happen if it is not natural?

Answer: Because of your ignorance. You have free will and you can use your free will against life. If you use your free will against life it is unnatural because you are not in coordination with the divine laws. You are shifting, destroying the rules, the regulations, the laws of Nature.

Question: Does not good come out of this in the world?

Answer: Unreality makes you unreal. Unreal things cannot continue to exist. Gold can exist in fire; "straw" cannot. It is better to love than hate. It is better to give than to steal. It is better to spread beauty than ugliness. It is better to make people honest than criminals.

Question: I always thought it was part of God's plan in each of us that everything here was a reflection of a greater realm.

Answer: My goodness, God told you to love each other. Are you loving? Do not go too far. Love each other. There is no greater love than the love that a man gives his life for others. That is God's advice. Why are you cheating yourself? Everything you do against God's command means you are cheating yourself.

People still say that was God's plan for me. They kill others for their selfish interests and say, "God wanted me to do that." People destroy their own intellect, heart, and body and say, "That was the will of God." What a self-deception. Such people need lots of painful experience to awaken them from their own sleep.

There are two kinds of reality for people. One is that you see with your own eyes a tree and water nearby, and you go and sit under the tree and drink from the water. Second you see a mirage and you say, "With my own eyes I see it," but you never prove that it is there, when you see it. That is unreality and self-deception.

On the spiritual journey you advance only by proving to yourself that you are not falling into self-deception.

Each step on the path leads you to greater reality, until you see yourself as you are, as you can be.

5

Building the Soul with Love

The sun we see in the heavens is a trinity.

1. It has Light, which is the origin of intellect.
2. It has Love, which is the origin of the human soul.
3. It has Energy, which is the origin of human will-power.

This triple sun consists of the sun, the Heart of the Sun, and the Central Spiritual Sun.

It is true that each human being on earth is created by the sun and is a son of the sun.

For millions of years, human Sparks have been nourished by the sun. Through a long and arduous evolution, living forms were gradually endowed with human intelligence. Every life-form, including man, is essentially space, lacking individuality, operating by push buttons, by incoming impressions and reactions. Slowly, this space individualizes and builds up as the human soul — which is the individual born out of space. Now man exists; before he had no existence.

What makes a person continue his existence? The answer is that accumulated deeds, words, actions, emotions, reactions, responses, thoughts, and dreams which unite with a common frequency come back into incarnation through a human form — which may or may not have a soul. It is from the moment of building the soul that man has individuality, and from this moment on he is the one who incarnates, propelled and carried on by his past action on three levels, or by his karma.

When the soul is built enough as an individuality, he initiates a destructive process toward those elements that automatically control the process of death and rebirth. From that moment on he is on the path of liberation and has continuity of consciousness, on earth and on the subtle planes. He is an existence which has freedom to cooperate with the creative forces of Nature.

It is the task of the Solar Angel to engineer and orchestrate the person in such a way that the Inner Temple is eventually constructed.

Humanity must pass through three stages of development to be truly a son of the sun. It must first develop intellect. Secondly, it must develop the soul and become a soul. In the third stage, it must develop will.

At present we are at the second stage. The majority of humanity, consciously or unconsciously, is engaged in developing the human soul. The third stage has not been reached except by a few individuals like Lord Buddha, Christ, and a few others.

How can the human soul be developed?

The human soul develops only through the use of the energy of the Heart of the Sun, which is called Solar or Love energy. Throughout millions of years, man tries to love; and as he loves, he becomes a human soul.

Every thought based on love, every word and relation, any action based on love builds the human soul. Drop by drop, atom by atom, the human soul is constructed.

Just as the sun is triple in nature, so is the solar system. The first solar system was nourished by the Light, or intellect, of the Sun. The second solar system is nourished by Light, with the addition of Love. Light builds the body; Love builds the soul. The source of nourishment for the second solar system is Love from the Heart of the Sun.

The third solar system will be nourished by Willpower. In the third solar system, the Central Spiritual Sun will be the source of nourishment.

People must be educated to understand the energy of Love as the builder and the energy of the human soul. The human soul is love, and as it reaches perfection, Love will be perfect and the human soul will be the embodiment of Love.

The human soul will not become perfect as "the Father in heaven [the Sun] is perfect" until it develops the Father's Willpower.

We do not know what Willpower is yet. We have a few ideas given to us by Those Who were able to build Their souls and cultivate Willpower before They entered the third solar system.

The real duty of a human being at this time is to be a soul. To do this we must attract the energy of the Heart of the Sun through our hearts. This is what the energy of Love is. The Heart is the Magnet of Love energy. Unless one unfolds his heart, he cannot love or accept love.

In being transferred from the first solar system to the second, people have become so identified with their intellect that they cannot understand that Love can do all that the intellect does — and more. Very soon, great Teachers will come and educate humanity about the powers of Love.

Love can know, can analyze, synthesize, discriminate, choose, create, discover, and penetrate more deeply than intellect. Love can see all possible relationships in the past, present, and future. Love is free from glamor, illusion, and past-crystallized memories. But we do not try to use this energy.

Love performs one hundred times better than the light of intellect, and additionally, it unifies, harmonizes, and synthesizes where the intellect may not. Love energy is still in its infancy.

When the Great Ones reveal the nature of Love to us, we will start living as souls instead of as physical bodies, emotions, and thoughts. When we develop Love, we will be able to understand situations instantaneously and most accurately. Through Love we will be able to free ourselves from all attachments, which will enable us to touch the heart of all living beings.

There is an intellectual way to try and solve the mysteries of creation and bring health, happiness, and prosperity. But because the intellect cannot work constructively until Love energy is active, it always contradicts itself — and while building ladders of survival, it falls into the danger of annihilation. In Love, there is no contradiction. There is only balance, equilibrium, and a clear understanding of events.

In the third solar system, the human soul will work to be a Spiritual Triad of Light, Love, and Power — eventually becoming the Self, or the Son of the Sun.

All that stand against love, against the Magnet of the Heart, are destructive elements that reduce the human soul until man eventually becomes a soulless machine.

In this age, many are losing their souls and many are building their souls. As the human soul is built, thirteen powers of the human soul gradually emerge. We call them higher senses which operate in the higher mental, Intuitional, and Atmic Planes. They are called

1. Spiritual discernment
2. Response to group vibration
3. Spiritual telepathy
4. Comprehension
5. Healing
6. Divine vision
7. Intuition
8. Idealism
9. Beatitude
10. Active service
11. Realization
12. Perfection
13. Omniscience

The higher mental, Intuitional, and Atmic Planes form a field of electrical energy that is called the Spiritual Triad. The human soul eventually focuses itself at the center of the Triad and uses the above-mentioned senses. We are told that conscious immortality cannot be experienced until the human soul focuses itself at the center of the Spiritual Triad.

The Spiritual Triad shines as a Sun with Its own triple power: intelligence, pure love, and willpower. The human soul achieves such a lofty level of beingness in experiencing pure love and building itself up. Love — which is the energy of the Heart of the Sun — is the substance from which the human soul is constructed.

Every creature will eventually realize that individuality is achieved only through loving the lower self — through living, moving, and having existence in Love.

6

Soul and Plan

When we think about the relation of man to the macrocosm, we see that the whole existence of man is nothing else but an idea projected out of the Cosmic Mind and eventually materialized on the objective plane.

Similarly our ideas and thoughtforms are beings, conceived by us, which have their life and existence and objectification in the material plane.

Every creative act passes through three major stages: One is the *purpose*, next comes the *plan*, next comes the *objective existence.*

The purpose in man is expressed as the Monad, the Divine Spark. The plan is expressed as the human soul. The objective existence, or objectification is expressed as the threefold personality.

The purpose tends to become the plan on the way of actualization, and the plan tends to become the personality to fulfill the purpose.

In this process the purpose tries to individualize and become a living, acting, self-determined man. After he individualizes and discovers that he is a separate being in the Universe he begins to shift his direction and strive toward conscious unity with the whole. In the process, the personality tries to be the soul, and the soul tries to be the Self. The personality recognizes the plan behind all that the personality was built for. And the plan recognizes the source of its existence striving toward the purpose. Thus, the consciousness of the individualized being unifies in itself — manifestation, the plan, and the purpose behind the plan.

On the path of return, the personality cannot survive unless it understands the goal of its existence, and gradually it discovers that the goal of its existence is to give expression to the plan hidden within him, or to let the soul manifest himself through his body, emotions, and mind.

The soul, the human soul, has in himself the plan which is the way the man should conduct his life in the three worlds. His success depends on knowing the plan and living the plan.

After the plan, or the soul is actualized, man begins to see his *Self* — the core of his soul which makes him realize the why of everything that is going on in the three worlds.

Knowing and living in the consciousness of purpose is the process by which man develops his Divine Self — his individualized Divine Self Who is aware of the existence of the All Self.

The human soul is like a bud of a lily which gradually opens. Each stage of opening of the bud of the soul introduces various changes in the life of the personality in the world of activities, emotions, and thoughts.

The process of unfoldment of the human soul depends on the discipline, purification, and integration of the physical, emotional, and mental natures of man.

When the threefold personality, which is the field of activity, is organized, purified, and highly aligned with the plan, the Rays of the soul radiate out unobstructed.

7

Soul Infusion

The human soul is the *light* and *love* and *will power* in the personality according to the level of evolution of the personality.

Physical, astral, and mental bodies form the personality until it is integrated by the light, love, and will of the human soul.

The integrated personality is the fruit of the labor of the human soul. The Ray of the human soul conditions the aspects of the soul.

The First Ray gives enlightenment and willpower.

The Second Ray gives enlightenment and love power.

The Third Ray gives enlightenment and light power.

Having these Ray qualities does not mean that they manifest one hundred percent in the soul. The evolution of the soul determines the degree of manifestation of the power of the three Rays.

Our three bodies have their own light, love, and power, depending on their evolution, but they are not coordinated and integrated until they become one personality.

The factor that makes cooperation between the Solar Angel and the human soul possible is the personality. As the personality forms and sublimates, the human soul gains the right to be fused with the Solar Angel.

The labor of the human soul makes him worthy to fuse with the Soul — Solar Angel — and gain the right to Soul-infusion.

Cooperation between two points is possible through a common vision, goal, or purpose. In this case the personality, Solar Angel, and human soul work together to focus the personality, as the vehicle for light, love, and power, and as an instrument of service in the three lower worlds.

Soul-infusion is called in the Ageless Wisdom the marriage in heaven. Our health, our success in life, the power of our intelligence, our progress on the path, and also the influence we project upon life depend upon Soul-infusion.

In the process of Soul-infusion there are terms which need clear definitions:

1. Body or vehicle
2. Spark
3. Ego
4. Human soul or soul
5. Spiritual Triad
6. Solar Angel, Transpersonal Self
7. Transcendental Self
8. Man
9. Lower self
10. Personality

1. *Body or vehicle* is organized matter ensouled by an elemental, built on a specific plan to manifest a specific purpose. We have several bodies; each of these fulfills a purpose.

The purpose of the physical vehicle is to make the man know about the physical world, to make him relate with it and bring changes within it according to the intentions or the plan of a higher Entity. The same applies to the emotional and mental bodies with their corresponding spheres. These three bodies also act as refineries.

The mental body is a living organism, spread all over our body and condensed around our head. The emotional body is another living entity surrounding our body. It has its own centers and energy lines. The etheric body is a coil of energies surrounding and penetrating the physical body. It has seven main centers, and it is the vehicle which absorbs prana from the sun and transmits it to the physical body.[1]

2. *Spark* is the fiery primordial atom that radiated out from the Central Fire. The Spark is the seed of life in which the image of Cosmos exists.

The human Spark is the real identity of man which, after traveling through the lower kingdoms eventually built the human body.

The Spark is the possibility in man, the source of life, growth, and progress. The Spark is identified with matter as the life principle of matter.

Each of us is a Spark related to our Source through a thread of light. This thread of light is the extension of the Spark. It is part of the Spark which eventually will be the path through which the Spark will travel back to Its Source. That is why we are told that man is the path itself. "I am the path." He is the path and the traveling Spark.

1. See *New Dimensions in Healing* for further information on the three bodies and centers.

The Spark is the real man. It is an extension of a Ray which hits the physical substance and slowly organizes the physical life, then the emotional and mental life, thus withdrawing Itself up to the mental, then intuitional, and higher levels.

The Spark has different names on Its path of development. For example, when It is really captured in the physical body and totally identified with it, we call It the "sleeping spark," or the reflection. When It awakens and wants to be aware of Its powers and destination, we call It the "pilgrim."

When It arrives on the mental plane and has highly organized the three bodies — mental, emotional, physical-etheric — we call it a "personality."

When it further advances and harmonizes all Its activities in the light of the Inner Guide, we call It the unfolding human soul.

When It releases the Solar Angel and stands on Its own, we call It a Soul or an Arhat.

When It advances to higher realms, we call it the Spiritual Triad, then the Self or the Monad or the Divine Spark.

3. *Ego* is the Spark identified with the vehicles. We have the

- Physical ego
- Emotional ego
- Mental ego
- Personality ego

The ego is always the separative, selfish, self-seeking power in man. The physical ego plays with urges and drives. The emotional ego plays with glamors and desires. The mental ego enjoys illusions, superstitions, prejudices, separation, vanity, and pride.

4. The *human soul* or *soul.* When we write Soul with a capital "S," it refers to the Solar Angel. When it is written with a small "s," it refers to the human soul.

The human soul is a general term, and it denotes all the stages of development of the Spark, beginning with the moment It entered human evolution and ending at the Seventh Initiation.

But if we say "soul," it has a specific meaning. The Spark during Its development eventually realizes that It is not the physical body, not the emotional body, not the mental body. It is aware that It is an independent entity using the lower vehicles as the channels of Its communication with the three worlds. We call this stage of the progressing Spark, "soul."

The Spark is like a photographic negative on which the Self gradually comes into existence as the image of "God." The soul is an advanced stage of such a development.

One becomes a soul when he radiates the twelve virtues of the Inner Lotus and, through fusion with the Solar Angel, he gives birth to himself, as a soul.

The soul now enters superhuman evolution. He is an Arhat, one who renounced selfhood and is proceeding toward the All-Self. An Arhat radiates the rays of twelve virtues with their specific colors. Each ray is a path toward higher sources of wisdom, beauty, and power.

An Arhat walks in the Hall of the Triangle — in full freedom.

5. The *Spiritual Triad* is the next stage of the Spark. The human soul graduates from the mental plane and enters the vortex of light which is formed by the energy field radiated out from the Mental, Intuitional, and Atmic Permanent Atoms; he uses the higher mental plane and the intuitional and atmic vehicles as vehicles of higher contact and as vehicles of expression upon those planes.

In this stage the human Spark or soul not only knows that he is not the physical, emotional, and mental bodies, but he is also able to stand out of these bodies and act as a liberated entity. He is able to stand aside from his physical, emotional, and mental bodies and act in the space as a liberated soul, with pure light, love, and power.

6. *Solar Angel,* Transpersonal Self, is the Inner Guide, the Inner Teacher who is not part of the Spark but a visitor who enables the Spark to proceed on the path of evolution.

The Solar Angel was, once upon a time, a human being who passed all the initiations and became a *Nirvani*, which means one who achieved liberation from the human kingdom.

The Solar Angel is like a magnetic bridge which life after life draws the Spark to Itself. A moment comes when the human soul, before passing on to the Spiritual Triad, fuses with the Solar Angel and for a while works as one. When the human soul passes on to the Spiritual Triad at the Fourth Initiation, the Solar Angel leaves him and continues Its Solar progress, or engages Itself with a newly born human being from lower kingdoms.

The Solar Angel is a great entity who finished Its cyclic development in previous solar systems and came to help the evolution of humanity. This happened in the Lemurian Race. The Solar Angel came and entered the human aura.

There are many esoteric traditions, as well as witnesses in the fields of psychology, poetry, and others who state that there is something besides the human being in man, something which gives inspiration, light, direction, and great leadership. Sometimes It totally dominates the man and expresses Itself. Some of us have had this experience.

It has been found that there is something greater in man, something that in a moment may take control and express greater wisdom and beauty. We have had these experiences, and we are going to have deeper experiences. Slowly and scientifically we are going to work toward our future and contact the Inner Guide, our Inner Leader.[2]

The mental body is the vehicle through which the Solar Angel expresses Itself. Then we have the emotional body, the physical-etheric body, and the reflection. This reflection lives for ages and ages in the "soil," in the earth of the physical body. There is no communication with the Solar Angel, no knowledge of being the Divine Spark. Man is lost in the body; he lives wholly as the physical body.

When he lives on this level, his greatest instinct is self-preservation. He fights, he kills, he does many things just to preserve that body; he uses anger and greed because the body is very important for his future evolution. The three main instincts of the reflection, when it is totally identified

2. There is a vast difference between the Solar Angel and obsessing entities. See *Obsession and Possession* and *The Solar Angel.*

with the physical body, express themselves as anger, greed, and self-preservation.

7. *The Transcendental Self* — or the Self. When the Spark enters the Monadic and Divine Planes and realizes that It is one with the One Self in Nature, we call It the Self. The Self is a full-bloomed Spark, and in the Spark shines the image of God — "I and my Father are one." God and Father here refer to the One Self.

8. *Man* is a term used to refer to all these stages. In particular, man is divided into the following stages:

- Aspirant
- Disciple
- Initiate
- Arhat
- Master
- Chohan
- Resurrected One

These are all stages of the Spark, as far as our solar system is concerned.

The purpose of the Self is to demonstrate His beauty through all levels and through all bodies.

9. *Lower self* is another term used in esotericism to refer to the sum total of the physical, emotional, and mental bodies in which the human Spark is trapped.

10. The *personality* is the integrated sum total of the physical, emotional, and mental elementals. If it is spelled

with a capital "P," it refers to the Spark or the human soul, acting as the personality.

There is another term used in some esoteric and psychological works. It is "sub-personality." Sub-personality is a complicated term. It means forces which are running the show behind the personality; or your former personality which is still active; or maya, glamor, illusion strong enough to control your personality vehicles.

Posthypnotic suggestions often act as sub-personalities. Strong impressions manifest as sub-personalities. It is also possible that obsessing entities act as sub-personalities.

Through suffering and experience the reflection slowly starts to awaken. First a communication line is established between the physical and emotional bodies. Here the man feels at times wholly physical, sometimes wholly emotional, and sometimes a mixture between the two. According to the circumstances and according to the cycles of the sun, the moon and other influences, man alternates between his physical and emotional bodies and does not use his mind at all. He has no connection with it yet.

When the man, the reflection, slowly pulls himself up from physical attachment and identification, he expresses two qualities in the emotional body — attachment and desire. These are the great instincts of the emotional body. At the same time, he has not lost the physical body instincts of greed, anger, and self-preservation. He has them, and he uses them in the light of his desires and attachments. Thus his greed is ten times more; his anger is equally increased; and he desires more than ever to preserve his life.

Through the passing ages, the reflection steps on another path through the mind. The reflection is going back Home. This is the path of the Prodigal Son who is going back to his Father. However, when he enters the mental plane he expresses selfish, separative, and harmful characteristics. Immediately upon entering this plane he experiences himself as being different from all other human beings. He says, "I am." He does not care for others, but does everything possible to continue the preservation of his physical and emotional life through greed, anger, desire, and attachment along with the newly added protection of the intellect.

Now he has ways and means to create mentally such conditions which will safely keep his body, satisfy his desires, and continue his attachments. The mind serves all these things; the mind becomes the slave of the emotional and physical instincts. In addition, in the mind the man discovers pride.

On this long journey, the two greatest lessons of Nature are pain and wisdom. On his way, eventually this reflection going homeward meets advanced people who tell him that what he is doing is not right. This is wisdom. He receives advice, reads books, attends lectures. He thinks and says it is good, and yet he wants to go on doing as he has always done.

He begins to pass through painful experiences. He conquers. He fails and is conquered. He beats and is beaten. He hits and is hit. Through all these laws and forces, Nature leads him to the light of the Solar Angel.

When pain and wisdom teach him enough, then he begins to see the two great poles. The lives of his physical, emotional, and mental bodies pull him in one direction; the life of his Solar Angel pulls him in another direction. This is the beginning of the greatest conflict in a man's life. The physical body says "greed." The Solar Angel says "renounce." The emotional body says "hate." The Solar Angel says "love."

The man recognizes and senses some kind of good, but he is still attached to pride, greed, selfishness, and desires. The physical body says, "Protect these things." The Solar Angel says, "Take them and destroy them."

The man is torn between two extremes, two opposing viewpoints. This is the "monkey" period of life. In other words, he recognizes the good and yet uses life for his lower self.

The Solar Angel then, in various ways and means, awakens him so that he comes to understand what is right and what is wrong. He begins to heed the hints and suggestions from the light of his Soul.

During this period the man slowly learns to use seven different methods to facilitate his response to the impressions and call of the Solar Angel. These are

1. Detachment-renouncement
2. Aspiration
3. Purification
4. Discipline
5. Meditation
6. Selfless, sacrificial service
7. Group work

Through the use of these seven methods, the man progressively, through conflict and striving, increases the sensitivity of his vehicles so that he may respond to the need as expressed by the Solar Angel.

There are many different ways in which the Solar Angel can communicate with the reflection. It can send messages through symbolic dreams, by direct telepathy, or by warning sounds. The Solar Angel is able to send men, books, and objects in order to help the man see and inspire him with the ideals of purity, greatness, and beauty. The Solar Angel can appear to him and give him direct instructions, or take him to Ashrams and Masters' classes. These are some of the ways the Solar Angel can aid the human being on his journey Home.

And what is the result of all this? Slowly the human Spark approaches and finds Its position at the center of the life of the Solar Angel. It is like a newborn baby, and the Solar Angel loves It like a mother. This is called the "new birth." Man is born. He is now not flesh; he is not the emotional body; he is not the mental body; but he has a new birth that is in light, love, power, group consciousness, purity, and trust.

Very slowly the man fuses with the intention of the Solar Angel. The day comes when the child marries with the Soul. In all literature this is called the "marriage in heaven with the Bride." In the Song of Solomon, for example, we read, "Where are you, my dearest? I want to marry you." This is the Spark of the human being who is searching for the great beauty, to marry and be one with that beauty, the Solar Angel.

There is a wonderful story from the *Mathnawi* of Rumi which says: There was a lover who went to visit his beloved.

He knocked on the door and the girl answered, "Who is it?"

"It is I," he replied, "your friend."

"I am sorry," she answered, "there is not room for you in here."

The boy was confused, and after trying various methods to gain admittance, he understood that his beloved expected him to realize a great truth. So once more he returned and knocked on her door. The girl asked, "Who is it?"

This time he replied, "It is you."

"Well," she exclaimed, "then you may come in."

This is how the Spark becomes fused with the Solar Angel in spiritual marriage.

Just as individuals are in different stages, so are nations. One can see their lights; one can see which nations are in their physical bodies expressing greed, anger, and self-preservation; which are in their emotional bodies expressing attachment and desire along with anger, greed, and self-preservation; and which are in their mental bodies adding pride, separateness, and selfishness to these other qualities.

You can also see which nation is tuning in with its Solar Angel as a group. As you watch throughout your lifetime, you can observe which nation is acting in real group consciousness; which nation is knocking on the door of the Solar Angel. When the national Solar Angel is contacted, then in the consciousness of that nation there will be seen only one Goal — the unity of all human beings and their highest good.

The results of Soul-infusion for the human being and for the group and nation are pure love, light, and power. All qualities of the lower planes are changing into the ideal of the welfare of the whole. At the same time, there is joy, a sense of responsibility, and purposeful living. Fusion with the Solar Angel releases great creativity and fearlessness. The Soul-infused personality or nation understands the beauty and meaning of sacrifice, simplicity, trust, and courage.

When the individual, group, or nation becomes fused with the Solar Angel, there is the power to affect the environment in new ways. Where there is conflict, this fusion has the power to establish harmony; where there is ignorance, it can reveal freedom; where there is sickness, it can heal. A Soul-infused being is able to reorient other beings toward the light of the Solar Angel.

One of the greatest achievements of man is Self-mastery. This is the state of consciousness in which man is himself and is the master of all his vehicles and the mechanical reactions to the environment, to the inner and outer worlds. This is the goal man must achieve. We are told that in the Aryan Age[3] man must be able to master himself on the mental plane and strive toward mastery on the Intuitional Plane.

The way leading to such achievement is the way in which the Spark learns to identify with the Real Self and leave the not-self behind. It is known that a man's identification, his sense of himself, changes every moment. These passing selves are only the vehicles he uses and the vehicles with which he identifies.

Man's goal is to strive toward the changeless Self within the vehicles. This Self is his Self. The challenge for each man, each group, and each nation is to be ever-awakening, ever-

3. The term "Aryan" refers to the present period of development of the human race.

becoming, ever-unfolding in greater Self-mastery and Self-actualization.

Soul-infusion takes place gradually as maya, glamors, illusions, and the Dweller on the Threshold are conquered.

One cannot directly come in contact with the sun until the dust, fog, pollution, and clouds are removed. Soul-infusion proceeds as the aura of man is purified and the inner Sun is contacted.

Maya is the unsatisfied urges and drives of past lives, accumulated in the etheric body and in the lower centers. It controls our physical body in such a way that we can hardly exercise control over it. Each maya highly charges the nature of the forces received by the astral body.

Glamor is the identification with the objects of our desires. Whenever we are identified with an object of our desires we build a replica of the object of our desire in our astral body. The average man is loaded with such objects, and that is why his astral sensitivity and his emotional relationships are so distorted.

Each glamor and each maya control the energy flow and channel it toward their ends.

Illusion is distorted images of facts or truths. The root of illusion is separatism. As long as man lives as a separate entity with separate interests, he cannot see the things as they are; so he changes and translates things from the point of his individual interests.[4]

When our minds are full of illusions we cannot translate clearly the incoming impressions, and we distort them.

4. For detailed discussion of the three qualities, please see *Challenge for Discipleship.*

In most cases people communicate with each other through their illusions rather than through their Selves.

The *Dweller on the Threshold* is not formed or active until the Third Initiation, at which time the human soul awakens to his own inner Divinity and his purpose is revealed to him. He sees himself as the future king, as the future Self. The Dweller on the Threshold is the personality, is the collective elemental of the physical, emotional, and mental elementals with which he was identified for millions of years. When the collective elemental feels that the human soul is gaining greater freedom and becoming ready to control and master them, it prepares itself to block the path of ascent of the human soul.

The passage for the soul is through the etheric, astral, and mental bodies, and the gate is found on the top of the head. Through this gate the human soul enters the electrical field of the Spiritual Triad.

Elementals are lives and they enter the path of evolution if the human soul enters the path of initiation. The human soul acts as a Solar Angel to the elementals, as the Solar Angel is toward the human soul.

Elementals are natural entities, but the human ego degenerates them through wrong activities, emotions, and thoughts, filling them with the pollution of maya, glamor, and illusions. When one lives in maya, glamor, and illusion, he deprives the elementals of light and prepares for himself future troubles.

Elementals behave mechanically. They are like computers: they work out the programming put into them by the developing human soul or ego.

Soul-infusion is the period in which the formation of the human soul takes place. When Soul-infusion is completed, the human soul comes into being as a rising Sun. It is this Sun that brings beauty to the world, spreads fragrance, and becomes a path of achievement for others.

8

Personality and Soul

Let us discuss personality reaction and soul reaction and the difference between them. This is a very important subject and it is very practical.

First of all I want to explain what the personality is really. It is your reaction, it is your expression, it is your radiation that builds whatever you are. For example, physically you react to the light. It is that reaction that conditions the beauty, the materials, the substance of your body. Then there are your emotional reactions. Let us say that you are loving, you are joyful, you are peaceful, and you are beautiful. When you react in this way, you create an astral body, the emotional body, that is very high quality. When you react mentally to justice, to beauty, to truth, to freedom, to joy, you build a certain kind of mental body that is very high quality.

But if you are reacting physically in a way that destroys the physical body, you will have a very weak physical body. If you are reacting with anger, jealousy, revengefulness, and hate, you build an astral body that is very vulnerable, stagnated, dangerous, and many, many germs and microbes leak into that body. Also mentally, if you are reacting unrighteously, you are always on the false side, the deceptive side. You are falsifying things, you are not trustworthy, you are in vanity, you are always angry, and you are always cruel. These kinds of things build a mental body that is weak, destructive, and criminal.

So when I say that your reactions build you, that is what I mean. For example, if you radiate love, you build a loving body. If you radiate truth, you build a body that occupies or produces or creates truth. If you react physically to the laws of Nature, you build your physical body. But when you live a life against the laws of Nature, you destroy your physical body, not only in this incarnation but also in coming incarnations.

I wanted to make this so clear because it is one of the great foundations.

What is personality? Personality is the combination of your physical, emotional, and mental natures. Your physical body is really healthy and beautiful. Your emotional body is organized. If your mental body also is organized and these three are working in unison, as a complete unity, we call it "personality."

We do not have many who are personalities. People think that they have personality but they do not have it. Maybe twenty percent of humanity or thirty percent has personality. But we have the possibility of these three natures that we call personality, which is written with a little "p."

Because you have a physical nature, you react physically to the environment. You have an emotional nature and you react emotionally. You have a mental nature and you react mentally. Or we say that you have a personality reaction because it is combined physically, emotionally, and mentally. But it is not necessarily personality. To be a personality is whatever you think, you feel and act. Whatever you feel, you think and act. Whatever you act, you feel and think. It is combined. It is simultaneous. It is in unison. We call such a man an integrated personality. It is very clear that the physical mechanism, the mental mechanism, and the emotional mechanism act as one gear. The gears are working — physically, emotionally, and mentally — as one.

But if you say that this is not always the case because sometimes your mind thinks something and your emotions do something else and your body does not care either for your thoughts nor your emotions, though you have these three bodies we call this a split personality or not a personality yet. For example, you decide something. A few minutes later an emotion comes and says, "I don't want to do it." So you are not yet a personality. Or mentally and emotionally you agree, but the physical body says, "I am lazy." It does not obey.

When the physical body obeys the urges and drives of the emotional body with mental direction, we say that the man is developing into a personality. He thinks, he feels, he does simultaneously. Also, this stage is a little dangerous for you because the physical plane immediately spreads to the emotional level and the mental plane. That is why disciples feel pain not in the physical body only. The pain is in three dimensions.

When a man is not cooperating and is not integrated, his pain is only in the physical body or his pain is only in the emotional body. Or he feels pain only in the mental body.

There is no connecting link yet. But when he becomes a personality, any pain, any joy immediately spreads. For example, if he is a very integrated personality, when you touch his physical body, emotionally and mentally he reacts.

Some animals, for example, when you put a needle in them, they do not even move because they do not feel it. There are also human beings who do not feel emotionally or mentally even when they have suffering and pain in their physical body.

This is a great science and a great subject. But for the purpose of this chapter it is better to know the fundamentals — that when the physical body, emotional body, and mental body are acting in unison, when they are acting as one mechanism, we say that the man or woman has a personality.

Now what is the soul reaction? This is also a very strange, very beautiful Teaching that is given by great, great Sages. According to this Teaching man is a Spark of that Almighty Power, and like that Power in his own degree he creates, destroys, regenerates, and heals, and again builds.

Every phenomenon in Nature, every form in Nature has a Core, has a kernel. If there is no kernel nothing remains. For example, if you take away the kernel of man, which is his soul, he disintegrates. There must be something that holds the body and its activity together. For example, I am here talking. Who is doing that? It is the one that is in this body. If you take the one that is in your body out, the body does not exist. It disappears, slowly disintegrates.

You have, for example, a big company, a big nation. Each has its own kernel. Even a tooth has its kernel. We call these kernels, these Cores, the soul. And what is the soul? There are many, many misconceptions about the soul, from ordinary citizens to the so-called sages, yogis, and lamas. They do not know what they are talking about. A man in his Essence is a Spark of that Almighty Power. And this Spark gradually builds the body, the emotional body, and the mental body with the help of the constructive forces in the Nature. Everything can be built if there is a plan and if there is a focus to manifest that plan.

For example, a chair does not come suddenly and build itself, does it? Have you seen any construction in which the bricks fly and ten minutes later you have a house? That house is built by the soul of the house. Who is the soul? That soul is you.

The soul has a plan and knows how to adapt the material into that plan and build that form into a vision. You are the same thing. Your physical atoms and cells, emotional atoms, and mental atoms are drawn by a magnet that is you. This magnet draws them together and according to the plan that is in you he builds the body, he builds the emotional body, he builds the mental body and slowly, slowly develops them, sublimates them, transforms them.

How do you know that the one that is within you is not the body? It is very easy. You do not need to prove it because you say, "I want to move my hand," and you move it. And if you say, "I do not want to move my hand," the hand does not move. Because you have control, because you can reject or accept the movement of the body, we can say there is somebody in you that is not the body.

For example, I am walking. If I want to stop, I stop. The body cannot say to me, "Go," if I do not want to. Who is that that makes the body work, makes the body to lie down, makes the body swim and run or stop? That is what we are saying is the inner Core.

Okay, let us look at the emotional body. We may say that the Self does not exist. How does it not exist if I can reject my emotions, if I can love or hate, and if it is not my emotions that love or hate?

Similarly, you can think and you can stop thinking. You can create positive thinking or negative thinking — whatever you want. So it means that your mind is not you. There is somebody else behind the mind that is controlling and using the mind. Now that is the Divine Spark. That is your Self. But when we say Self and soul, we are not being accurate.

At first we have the Divine Spark — just like a little seed. A little seed falls into the ground, assimilates from the ground nourishment, eventually builds the stem, then the branches, then the flowers, then the leaves, and then slowly the fruit. It is just like that. You are the seed. These are the bodies that you are building.

When you are building your body, in the first stages the Spark is totally the slave of the body. At this point you do not have a self, almost It is sleeping. The body does anything it wants. Usually, as civilization and evolution proceed, the self, the Spark within you controls and masters your physical body.

Once you organize the body, you go to the emotional body and organize the emotional body, then the mental body.

These are the three stages in which you are graduating from physical, to emotional, to mental, and slowly, slowly controlling these three dimensions.

We say that we have an ego. Ego means the Spark identified with the physical, emotional, and mental natures. He does not know yet that he is an independent something. When he masters these three and is totally beyond the control of these three natures, he becomes a soul. He is not an ego anymore. That is why we say do not be an egotist. What does it mean? Do not work and live for your body, emotions, and mind. Be something greater than that. Become a soul.

When the soul progresses and enters into the Monadic Plane, an even higher plane, we say that man became a Self because he is totally in control of all the manifestations that he is using as his vehicles.

This information is necessary so that you will know what we are talking about when we are saying "soul," "ego," and "Self." People are totally confused about these terms.

What is the nature of the personality? The physical nature is greedy. It likes to possess and obsess and it searches always for its own happiness, sex, and food. If the Spark is lost in the physical nature, man has nothing and cannot improve. He is greedy. He wants to possess you. He wants to have food, sex, and enjoy the life. That is the physical. Man is reacting to the physical nature. He reacts to all life conditions in order to possess this, to have that, to create pleasures — sexual or food pleasures or greedy pleasures. He has nothing else. But once the Spark develops and comes to the emotional plane, he starts to control all the drives of the physical body.

When he enters into the astral body he has different drives and urges. What are they? Anger, hate, and fear are some of them. A man who is totally physical does not have anger, does not have hatred, does not have fear.

You bring two children here. One child has no fear. One child is fearful or is scared. Which one is more advanced? The one who has fear is more advanced because he fears himself. He is something and knows it. He knows himself. He is more conscious of himself and about the dangers that can happen. He develops fear, hate, and anger. Are these things bad? In that condition, they are not. You need fear to protect yourself. You need hate to keep yourself away from destructive purposes. You need anger to overcome obstacles. They are useful on that level.

When you come out of that level, you develop other things — vanity, separatism, and judgmentalism. Those people who have the Spark in their mind, or the Spark is functioning in the mental nature, have these three things. They are vain. That does not mean they are awake. They think they have everything, they can do everything, they are everything, and people will worship them because they are higher or lower as a man. Having vanity means they do not have yet the pure consciousness. That will come later if they become a soul.

They also are separative. They say this is mine, this is yours. They think in separative ways. You will see them react with vanity, separativeness, judgmentalism, or by deceiving people because they are short, fat, or lean; they have beauty or they do not have beauty; their nose is like this or like that. Such a person has the Spark in the mental plane, yet is not emancipated from the physical, emotional, and mental realms.

Let us now come to the soul. What are the qualities of the soul?

1. The soul is always oriented to group interest. The personality is only for his own ego. When he shakes hands with you, he thinks of what he can get from you. When he does some favor for you, he expects a reward for it. The soul is interested in the group's best interest. He says that even if he is going to lose, the group is going to gain. He says, "Let me do it so that the group, the organization, or humanity gains. "When I say "group" I do not refer to any immediate group. I refer to any group of people, any organization, any great nation, all of humanity. The whole human race is a group. Those who are souls in a group, they think in terms of the interest of that great group. Those who are personalities, they think in terms of how they can use this great group for their own advantage.

2. The soul is inclusive. He does not leave anything out. His thinking is inclusive, his feeling is inclusive, and his action is inclusive. If he does something physically, it must be something that is favorable for all. If he feels something, he feels everything in his feeling. If he thinks something, it is for the group. He thinks for all of them. If he thinks something that is only separative, he discards it. He has thoughts, emotions, and actions that are always inclusive. The personality is not inclusive. It is exclusive — we and you and them. We will take them and their positions because we must en-

joy the life. What about them? Who cares about it. That is the personality.

3. One of the greatest qualities of the soul is consideration. When a person is not considerate he is a personality. If he is considerate, he is a soul. "If I do this thing, what will happen to others?" That is being considerate. If I go at 1:00 o'clock at night to visit one of my friends, that is the personality. If you are a soul, you say, "They are sleeping, I must not do that."

Considerateness is one of the qualities of the soul. "If I drink this way, what reactions, responses will I create in that woman, that man? Let me consider." But if you say, "I don't care. Even if I come half naked, so what! This is a democratic country," you are not considerate. Why are you not considerate? Because you are not a soul yet. You are a personality.

4. The next quality is beauty. The soul always acts in beauty. His actions must be beautiful. His emotions must be charged with beauty. His thoughts must be beautiful. His motives and plans must be beautiful. But the personality does not care. The personality hurts your feelings, hurts the emotional body, hurts the physical body, hurts the mental body, destroys it, uses it, throws it out. He does not care. That is the personality.

5. The soul always obeys the foundation of justice. Let us say someone gossiped about me. Now let us take the soul reaction. Soul reaction says, "Watch your life. You did something wrong." "Yes, I did something wrong." He does not

care about what she is doing to him. He cares how he is going to react. He said, "Yes, I did something wrong. She gossiped about me but I can demonstrate love and respect and go and tell her thank you very much, you were right in saying these things and I myself beg your pardon." That is a soul reaction. A personality reaction says, "Who is that talking against me? I will gossip and use malice and slander to crush her." That is a personality relationship.

6. The soul is joyful. The personality is gloomy because everything scares the personality. He has things, he may do things, he has love, he may attract hatred, he is big, he is small. But for the soul there is no small. The soul does not increase or decrease. He is. He is always joyful because physically, emotionally, and mentally, he is not affected. He emancipated, liberated himself from these three things.

7. The soul has courage and daring. The personality defeats himself through false liberation. In any difficult time you see immediately whether that man is a personality or a soul. If he is a personality, he attacks the difficult problem as a personality and he defeats himself. He goes into depression from a sense of failure and gives up. But the soul is always courageous. His power is his courage, his daring. He knows that no matter how much he has lost, he can gain it again. Actually, the soul does not have a sense of failure or loss because immediately he withdraws himself from his physical, emotional, and mental natures and relaxes in Nirvana, in bliss.

8. The soul strives toward perfection. A personality strives to have, to feel, to possess, and to manipulate.

We have three stages of activity that can determine where we are. When we react to the light, we are in the personality. This is the first stage. Physically, emotionally, mentally, we have reactions of hatred, jealousy, revenge, vanity, separatism, and so on. This is all personality. We are reacting as a personality.

Then, we react sometimes as a soul, sometimes as a personality. We create a mess. In times of difficulty, we do the stupidist things. We talk nicely, then we curse. We dress beautifully, but we are stagnated inside. This is the second stage.

The third stage is soul reaction. When you see any action in life, when you are doing anything in life, catch yourself. Am I a soul here or a personality? Or do I mix it like a mule — half like a horse half like a donkey?

You can imagine certain conditions and see how you would act as a personality and as a soul. . Let us say that you are very happy. What would you do if you were a soul? What would you do if you were a personality?

For example, if you are a soul, you will take your happiness and make millions of people happy. If you are a personality, you will go and drink and do something wrong and ruin yourself. Happiness is a charge of energy. You can use it constructively or destructively. For example, ten million dollars came to you. If you are a personality, you will be very destructive, very selfish because you will be able to fulfill all those plans that you had in your life for your selfish ends. You fulfill them and manifest them. But if you are a soul, you will build a great hospital, build a great college, care for orphans. Do you see how they are different?

Every event in life tells you how you are going to act. Let us say you are a success. What will you do as a soul with success? What would you do as a personality? If you are successful and you are a soul, you will use your success only for the benefit of humanity. If you are a personality, all your success will be for the greater and greater status of your personality. You can see by how you act in your success — you are a personality or a soul. It is so important to be a soul in your life.

Let us say you failed... what will be your attitude and reaction to the failure if you are a soul? You will start again. You will prove only that you are "together." You will attack your problems again, you will stand up, you will not lose your goal, you will not lose your dreams and visions, and eventually you will again balance yourself and achieve prosperity and success.

What will be the personality reaction when you fail? First you will have depression, then hatred, anger, suicide, drinking, doping, and dying. A man came to me and said, "Torkom, there is nothing remaining in my life." "What are you talking about?" He was thirty-seven years old, a millionaire! "Torkom, nothing remains." "What happened to you?" He said, "I lost everything. It is gone. There is only one way," he said. "I am going home to shoot myself." I said, "Who made all the money?" "Well," he said, "I did." "Can't you make it again?" "No," he said, "it is gone." Now he is thinking as a personality. Do you understand what is happening? He is a complete failure.

Whenever you stand up and build again after a failure and achieve riches, new plans, you are smarter than before because you failed. You use your failure as a great lesson and do not repeat your mistakes again. You are wiser. That is the soul. If you are personality, you do not learn from your past failures and have as your greatest friend a bottle of whiskey.

So what does a spiritual man do if he fails and he is a soul? He examines the sources, the causes, the results, how it came about. And he tries to annihilate sorrow with joy. When you are in union with the soul, you are using the physical, emotional, and mental natures differently. When you are overcoming sorrow with joy, you are not damaging your physical, emotional, and mental natures. A Great Sage says that sorrow and depression bring such complicated diseases that no medical profession can help you. That is the personality. But the soul takes it as a joke. So what! It is very natural. So, if you have a disaster in the car and the whole family passes away, well, that was their karma. It could happen anytime. Who are you to judge? You are not capable of judging because only the personality judges. The soul is not there.

When you are mostly in hatred, when you have enemies and people hate you, what does the personality do? Immediately he hates back. Immediately he becomes an enemy. But Christ said something that was so interesting, "Love them that hate you." He knew that we should not be acting as a personality, but reacting as a soul. The soul loves; the personality hates.

Ungratefulness is another thing to watch for. We have seen many occasions when people are ungrateful. Did you do something great? You helped them — physically, emotionally, mentally — with advice and two days later they come and say, "Who cares about you? Who do you think you are?" They do not care about you. Wife goes to the husband, boyfriend goes to the girlfriend and says such ungrateful things. We are subjected to ungratefulness daily.

How does the personality respond? He says, "He didn't recognize me. He didn't even remember all the things I did." And he starts boiling and aching and killing himself. We are in that condition many times, right? What does the soul do? "Well, I did something good. I don't care if he remembers or not. I did it for the sake of doing good." That is the soul. Can you stand as a soul? But if you do not have soul, what will you do?

This is very practical. I do not want to speak anything here that you cannot use in your daily life. For me, metaphysics, Ageless Wisdom, religion must be really practical.

Today, immediately see how you are acting. Are you the physical body? Are you emotional, physical? Are you mental, physical, emotional? Or are you beyond that?

Discrimination immediately comes into your life when you observe your reactions. And do not forget one thing. It is not easy to understand so I like to repeat it. It is your reaction that builds you. It is not the condition of other people that builds you. It is your own reaction that eventually makes you what you are. So if your reactions are heart quality, you are together. You are physically, emotionally, and mentally yourself. You are a very high quality human being. This is the first lesson on the spiritual path. If you do not master these things, you do not need other metaphysical gymnastics.

Q&A

Question: Does stress exist for our soul?

Answer: No. It is the personality that goes through stress. Something is always called out. I saw this. A man, my Teacher, was very tense, working, always working and making everything beautiful. One day a big bomb exploded. That man immediately pulled himself from the personality and became a soul. He had the peace descend upon him.

Question: What part does the Solar Angel play in this?

Answer: Forget that. One of the great mistakes of people is just this. Teachers make a great mistake when they talk about what people cannot understand. It makes them hallucinate and become confused. If the student asks questions, the answer will not profit him. That is why in the ancient Pythagorean Brotherhood you must be five years silent until you build the foundation. Five years later you do not have questions anymore.

Question: Is it a mistake to let people go around taking things for granted?

Answer: Let them do anything they want because your attitude is to be indifferent. For example, let us say that I did something good for you. I would never think that you must come back and give something back to me. I am not doing it for expectation. I am doing it just like the sun. The nature of the sun is light, like my Teacher. It is radiation. He cannot do anything but radiate. We know that everybody's radiation here is either positive or negative. The sun does not care. That is a very big thing.

I am talking about this subject to create in your mind some opportunity that you can be this eventually. You will never forget it.

Question: How do you define love? And how would you distinguish it from attachment?

Answer: Love is not sex. Love is acting, feeling, thinking, doing, and planning for the welfare of others. This is love. Other than these, it is monkey business.

Somebody came to me and said, "Torkom , you are a masterpiece. The angels in heaven are watching you." I said, "What else?" "We worship you. You are this or that." I said, "That is enough, too much. My body is sick." Ten years later I said to him (he is a millionaire), "You know, we are painting this place. We need ten thousand dollars. Come on, express your love now." "You know," he said, "business is so bad." "You know," I said, "you were just flattering me back then. Now you can prove that you love me."

Love is not talk. It is not feeling. It is doing something, doing something for the welfare of the whole. That' is how you prove that you are loving. Nobody can love except if one is a soul. The other things are not love. They are excitement, beautiful legs, kisses, and sex. I am not saying they are bad. They are part of something. But love is beyond. When two people are here and they say, "We are going to marry." What can I say? She says, "I worship this man, Torkom."

One week later she says, "He is the devil." What kind of love is that?

Soul attitude does not change. Personality attitude changes. If the personality does say something, do not believe it because it will change five thousand times. The soul does not change.

***Question:** So if you make a decision, in order to make it last it must be as a soul?*

Answer: It must be a soul decision. The personality decides like this: Imagine that you go down to the seashore and you see beautiful legs. The physical body says, "she is beautiful," and you meet. Two days later you are not together because it was only a physical decision or maybe an emotional decision. Even a mental decision does not work. You sit down and meet a woman and she is so smart. And smartness has advantages, of course. She is so smart and you love her smartness and you say, "Because she is so smart, I want to marry her." That is a mental decision. You must look for something beyond smartness. When the soul decides, then there is no change.

***Question:** You were saying that during a catastrophe, sometimes it is good to be philosophical about it.*

Answer: Philosophical is a bad word. The correct word is calm.

You must learn the meanings of words. Colleges use that word without knowing the meaning.

Question: *What is the difference between calmness and a lack of caring?.*

Answer: Calmness understands and is interested in the welfare of others. Carelessness does not know and does not care. Calmness expands and evolves. If you are calm, magnetically you attract people. They come to you as a refuge. I have seen this. Whenever I am really calm, people come to me all day to cry to me. I reassure them with my calmness. But when I am not calm, they know it and they will not come.

That is the teaching for tonight. Always repeat this mantram that was given by the Tibetan Master, D.K. He says:

More radiant than the Sun,
Purer than the snow,
Subtler than the ether is the Self,
The spirit within my heart,
I am that Self,
That Self am I.

That is our destination. First become a personality. Then become a Soul-infused personality, which will be next, I assume. Then you will become the Self. Then that Self will grow and become the Soul of the Universe. That is a far ways off. But if you do not make a start, how are you going to grow?

9

Formation of the Human Soul

"No one who is not born from above is able to see the kingdom of heaven." [1]

This is a very profound statement which can only be solved esoterically. If one is not born from above he does not exist; he can see neither heaven nor earth.

"Above" refers to the Monadic Ray. The human soul is born through the individualization of the Monad in the womb of the Solar Angel. The Monadic Ray is " conceived" by the Solar Angel to give birth to the human soul. The human soul can gradually have the possibility to see the kingdom of God because he exists now and can grow and unfold. The "above" is the unconscious Ray, but the individualized soul has a chance to penetrate into the kingdom of God consciously and by the power of his merit.

"No one who is not born of water and of spirit is able to enter into the kingdom of God." [2]

Water in esoteric language refers to matter. Spirit is the Monadic Ray, while the Chalice, the womb of the Solar Angel, is the matter because it is built by deva substance.

---

1. John 3:5
2. *Ibid.*

The conceived Spark is taking birth of spirit and matter, or else he will have no existence, and he will not see the kingdom of God.

Also the word "see" does not refer to sight or perception. It means achievement, experience, realization. The human soul, when he is born in the womb of spirit and matter, can experience the kingdom of God and be a citizen of that kingdom.

In the course of centuries the Spark, with the help of the Solar Angel, developed various bodies with proper senses and conditions to be able to communicate with the life that is running on various planes.

The physical body, condensed from the etheric body, came into being. Then the astral body began to develop, then eventually the mental body began to develop. The creation of the bodies continues forever. Once a person enters into the Fourth Initiation, and focuses his consciousness in the Intuitional Plane, he lets the Solar Angel depart.

In esoteric books this is not clearly indicated. After the Solar Angel departs, the emancipated human soul, with the cooperation of the advanced devas of the mental, intuitional, and atmic bodies, begins to build his higher bodies to enable himself to communicate with even higher planes and eventually reach his glorious individuality, the Self.

It is a habit that we name people by the body they have. For example, an entity appears to us in a human body: he is a human being. If he appears to us in an astral body, he is an elemental. If he appears in an etheric body, he is a *Nirmanakaya*. Similarly if one developed his joy body, we call him a *Sambogakaya*, or if he has developed a power body we call him a *Dharmakaya.* We name people through the body in which they appear. But the point we must remember is that the real one always transcends the bodies.

The Self, according to his degree of unfoldment or control, builds bodies to communicate with the plane he is in. As he develops more experience, he builds higher bodies, or bodies that are able to communicate with a larger field of existence.

In the Cosmic Physical Plane, the highest body we know is called *Dharmakaya*, which in a sense means: the Being is aware of all Laws existing in the Cosmic Physical Plane. What a glorious and complicated apparatus it should be!

In *The Secret Doctrine* we read, "The archaic commentaries explain, as the reader must remember, that, of the Host of Dhyanis, whose turn it was to incarnate as the Egos of the immortal, but, *on this plane, senseless* monads—that some 'obeyed' (the law of evolution) immediately when the men of the Third Race became physiologically and physically ready, *i.e.*, when they had separated into sexes. These were those early conscious Beings who, now adding conscious knowledge and will to their inherent Divine purity, *created by Kriyasakti* the semi-Divine man, who became the seed on earth for future adepts".[3]

Only in *The Secret Doctrine* are these profound mysteries discovered. Man, being a Monad, was visited by Dhyani Chohans — in other words, Solar Angels Who were going to serve an ego, charging the "senseless Monad" or sleeping Spark of God in man with "conscious knowledge and will."

3. H.B. Blavatsky, *The Secret Doctrine*, Vol. II, p. 228. (Facsimile of Original Edition.)

Then the Monad was gradually trained to release Its inherent light, knowledge, and will power, and eventually be able to lead an independent life releasing the Ego — or Solar Angel — watching him, since the Third Race of Lemuria. But the most interesting point is that those who received the Ego before others, became semi-Divine beings through whom the future Adepts came into being. The *evolution* of the group who first received the host of Dhyani or Celestial Beings transcended those who did not receive or received them later — thousands or millions of years later.

The Hosts of Dhyanis, otherwise called Nirvanis or Solar Angels, kindled the lights in men in such a degree that on the path of the history of races, all leaders and saviors, kings and queens came from that group of people who received the Angels first.

Dharmakaya is like space. *Sambogakaya* is the sun in space. *Nirmanakaya* is the rainbow. The innate wisdom of *Dharmakaya* is that the *Dharmakaya* body is built of 10,000 Initiates of the ninth degree. *Sambogakaya* is built by initiates of the seventh degree. *Nirmanakaya* is built by fifth degree initiates.

We call them bodies — or vehicles, or groups, or organized beehives of souls who are in an advanced stage of development.

We are told that Buddha manifests in six realms:

1. Realm of gods — *Shakra*
2. Demi-gods — *Taksang*
3. Human — *Shakyamuni*
4. Animals — *steadfast lion*

5. Hungry gods — *flaming mouth*
6. Hell beings — *Dharma rga*

Nirmanakayas appear in four different forms:

1. Created Nirmanakayas as sacred images
2. Supreme Nirmanakayas — Buddha Sakymuni, who manifested as millions of Padma Sambhavas
3. Incarnated Nirmanakayas and Great Masters — Teachers
4. Variegated Nirmanakayas appearing in different forms

Nirmanakayas, Sambogakayas, and *Dharmakayas* are nothing else but vehicles of consciousness. As consciousness expands it builds higher bodies for expression and contact.

Some Buddhists say that the Monad is continuous. The Ageless Wisdom says that the mind is continuous but not the mental body, which is a device to express the labor of the mind. The continuous mind is called intelligence.

Intelligence, love, and willpower are three aspects of the human soul. These three aspects are continuous, and are in process of expanding. These three are manifested through the light of the soul, which we call *consciousness.*

In this sense, consciousness is continuous and unconditional beyond the threefold personality.

Wisdom is the synthesis of light, love, and power; in fact, wisdom is continuous as long as the balance of these three aspects continues.

The mind helps people to individualize. Wisdom or consciousness makes man fuse with the One Consciousness and act as that Consciousness. The difference between consciousness and wisdom is that wisdom is the practical application of the depth of consciousness.

Consciousness is the Buddha nature, the light that manifests through the soul.

10

The Soul and Psychology

If you sense an object, this means there is an object. But some people never think about the one who uses his sense to sense an object.

In *Bhagavad Gita* we read about the "Knower, the knowledge, and the field of knowledge."

If there is knowledge there must be a field of knowledge and a knower to know knowledge. This is so shockingly simple. In a few minutes of contemplation, you affirm your Self — the knower, the one that is the real you.

The Self can be contacted gradually. The first experience of Self is to know that you exist — as a person. You cannot have existence without having existence.

The second verification of Self is emotional. You feel this way, that way, but it is you who feels; a feeling does not exist without a feeler.

Then you verify the Self in the mental plane. You are not your knowledge, but you are the knower of knowledge.

The fourth level can be achieved through meditation and contemplation during which you let go your form, your feelings, and your knowledge, but to your surprise you discover that after all these are gone, you still exist. If you carry such a contemplation for a long time, you discover yourself quite apart from your physical, emotional, and mental bodies and all their furniture.

The Self can be discovered only by becoming the Self — the immortal, the ever-persisting, and ever-inclusive Core of your existence.

Certain psychologists confuse the Self — the real man — and the Guide within us. This is why they cannot solve many psychological problems existing between the Self and the Guide. The Guide, in occult books, is called the Guardian Angel or Solar Angel.

Some psychologists have another confusion; they think the Self in the human core is the Transpersonal Self, whereas the Transpersonal Self is the Solar Angel, not the human Self. The human Self is the Transcendental Self.

In the early stages of human evolution, the human being is the Solar Angel. It is the one Who uses the mechanism of man, according to the degree of the evolution of that mechanism. The human soul does not even exist, as in the early stages of evolution the man is the Monad and the Monad is not an individuality, but an abstraction, a Plane.

It is the Solar Angel that conceives the human soul by the fusion with the Monadic Ray, and the seed of the future human soul comes into being. In occult books this is called individualization.

Before a person is individualized, he is not a soul; he does not exist as an individuality.

Psychologists often meet the Solar Angel and think they have met the human soul. If all their techniques and attention are directed to a wrong address, they will fail.

The human soul must grow to a certain degree to respond to outer help, or else it is like trying to teach algebra to a baby who is not yet born. One of the important labors of the psychologist is to contact the human soul.

It is possible that when the human soul is not active yet, or is not born yet, the psychologist converses with those who are occupying different areas of the nature of man. These entities are so cleaver that they pretend they are the "person" himself, and fool the psychologist.

It is important also that a psychologist is a human soul. Only a soul can communicate with another soul. If a psychologist is like a diskette guided to help a person, he can come in contact with many thieves in the person and never with the human soul, the real owner of the mechanism.

People believe that a man can be trained to be a psychologist. This is almost an impossible task. A true psychologist is a mature human soul who understands what a human soul is, and how this soul behaves in various conditions and circumstances. If a psychologist is not a mature human soul his psychological help is artificial, and he has no key to unlock any door.

A mature human soul is naturally a psychologist. Before a man is a living soul, he is more like an animal. He cannot understand what the human being is. Of course, the animal can learn many things and be forced to do many things, but all that he does to help a person does not hit the target.

Because of the conditions of life, an awakening human soul has many complications in relation to the artificial life he has built for so many thousands of years. That person needs help, but only a psychologist who is himself a mature human soul can render that help.

So the psychologist is not built by information and training but by becoming.

The duty of the psychologist is to find the soul of the man. Many human souls are lost because of lack of care. A psychologist cannot help a person if he does not believe that he is a soul.

Many psychologists talk to the mechanism instead of the operator of the mechanism. They may correct the malfunction of the mechanism, but if the owner of the mechanism is not reached, he will again misuse the mechanism.

It is possible also that a psychologist, failing to contact the owner of the mechanism, puts artificial guards to operate the mechanism. These are posthypnotic suggestions which act like entities and do the job for a while until the owner of the mechanism begins to fight against them, causing great damage to the mechanism.

This situation is the same in education, and in many other fields of human endeavor.

The human soul must be recognized, contacted, and brought into freedom of life if we want to make the world a kingdom of souls.

The improvement of life begins with the awakening and formation of the human soul. It is the human soul who must be oriented to heal his mechanism, to strive toward the purpose of his life, and to create a life which provides all that is possible to reveal his glory.

No true help can be given to a human soul from a person who has no soul, or does not believe in the existence of a soul. A person who is a soul awakens the soul in others and challenges them to take control of their lives.

Some people regret their past failures and even cry for their failures with great sorrow. But some people, when they remember their failures, rejoice, because their souls made their failures the turning points of their life. They created crises in their life through which they made new breakthroughs toward higher dimensions.

The difference between these two attitudes is that the first one is still living caged in his memory. The second one, being an awakened soul, uses his failures to get closer to his Inner Core. When a person discriminates between failure and success, between expansion and contraction, he proves that his soul is awakening.

An absent soul has no discrimination. It is the Self, or the human soul, who draws wisdom from failure and builds his future success. We are told that an awakening human soul can use all events of life as stepping stones to reach the "other shore."

At certain times in meditation and sleep the human soul escapes his physical, emotional, and mental levels and involves himself with many experiences in the Other Worlds, experiences which he cannot transfer to the human brain except in very rare moments when the brain receives the experiences the human soul had in higher planes. These experiences are impressed on the mind on rare occasions.

Perseverance is another quality of the soul. Perseverance is the ability of the soul to strive toward his destination through all hindrances, obstacles, and difficulties of life. Perseverance makes the continuity possible.

All higher qualities stream from the human soul as rays from the rising sun.

11

Dying Souls

There are many, many souls that are dying. As you are living here your soul is dying and you do not know it. As you are in the astral or mental plane, it is possible that your soul is dying and you are not aware of it. The annihilation of the soul is a great explosion in the space. M.M. says, "Many, many souls are exploding in space." We call them aborted souls; they could not make it in the path in which they were developing.

The physical body can die millions of times but when the soul is in the physical body, physical death does not matter. Sometimes your physical death is a heroic one in that you are dying for something great for humanity. Your consciousness expands if you dedicate yourself more to the higher Common Good.

When I was reading the New Testament I found a jewel of a statement made by Christ: "Do not be afraid of those who kill your body, but be afraid of those who kill your soul." This means that the soul can be killed. Christ is giving a warning that we must be very careful of those who can kill our soul.

Killing the soul is of two kinds. One is that you yourself kill your soul. The other is that you let others kill your soul. People in the world are ninety-nine percent not interested in their soul. They are tremendously afraid of losing their body. This is the difference of thinking between people. In what percentage are you thinking about your soul and in what percentage are you talking, thinking, and worrying about your body? Most of humanity is worrying about its physical body: how to eat, how to make love, how to dress, how to have good homes. This is all important but if you are losing your soul, you do not have anything.

That brings us to the next saying of Christ which is related to the soul, "What do you benefit if you have all the world in your pocket, but you lose your soul?" You are finished, annihilated. What remains?

Actually people must start thinking about whether their soul is dying or whether their soul is unfolding, blooming, and reaching to its glory. These are two issues which must remain in your mind until you pass away.

After you pass away you will really see if you killed your soul, paralyzed it, or if you nourished your soul.

How We Kill Our Soul

We should have a badge which says, "What do you benefit if you gain the whole world but lose your soul?" It is something which every day must bug us. As you approach slowly, slowly to the coffin, think about it. Nothing will help you. That is the critical moment when you can have a little awakening and, for the next life, you will behave a little better if you did not paralyze your soul or make it really sick so that there is no chance for it to recover.

There are seven ways in which you can learn to kill your soul.

The killing of the soul or the dying of the soul starts every time you do something against your conscience, or you do something against the law of love and synthesis and unity, whether it hurts you or makes you happy. Every time you do something against your heart, you wound your soul. If you continue doing things that are against your heart and conscience, eventually you make your soul sick. When your soul becomes very sick and dies, you live as a corpse in this life, spreading the most contaminated radiations around you because you are dead but living. That is why Christ said, "Let the dead bury the dead." When Christ said, "Dead," He meant their bodies were alive but they were dead.

Living only for your body, pleasures, hatred, revenge, possession, and position kills your soul. It blinds you so that there is nothing else in the Universe. M.M. says, "When you go out at night, look at the stars".. We lose the vision because we are so occupied here with killing and hating each other or acting against our own conscience. It is so important to see. Every time you are totally engaged with your bodies and pleasures and hatred, possessions and positions, you lose your soul because you do not nourish it. It needs nourishment.

How do you nourish your soul? You nourish it by Beauty, Goodness, Righteousness, Joy, Freedom, Striving, Sacrificing yourself for human upliftment, not partial upliftment. Those who are awake know that humanity is one body and every time we are hurting one part we are hurting everything. This idea is for the future and needs perhaps two, three hundred years of suffering and pain and destruction so that we eventually understand what we are being told.

These ideas are floating in space and who can bring them down? Only those who are dedicated to the upliftment of humanity, or else these ideas will not come down. The Tibetan Master, speaking about something very interesting said, "Whenever Hierarchy wants to contact some galaxy, three Masters meditate, but if They are going to contact the Central Spiritual Sun all Hierarchy must be present. If They are going to contact Sirius or other galaxies, Shamballa must be present." In a united consciousness we can bring these great ideas down. If you have cleavages in your consciousness, in your mind, in your feelings there is a problem. I know that humanity now has that cleavage, "Yes. No. Do it. Do not do it. Peace. War." We are cleavages. That is why the Divine Help cannot come. Divine Help comes if we are focused.

What is it that focuses us against all these cleavages? Beauty focuses you, Goodness focuses you, Righteousness focuses you, Freedom focuses you, Joy focuses, Striving focuses you, heroic Service focuses you so that you are ready to dedicate yourself for something great for humanity. These transform you.

The Tibetan Master told about a man in Tibet who was working to survey the land. As this surveyor was doing his job, he suddenly saw that someone had fallen from a precipice five thousand feet below. The man said, "Let me go and bring him up," and he climbed down and was practically frozen as he brought the man up on his shoulders. As he came to the top, Great Ones came and took the survey to the Ashrams. They said, "Through your sacrifice you will be initiated into the mysteries of life."

You can kill your soul by wasting your time, body, energy on non-essentials. According to the Doctrine of Christ everyone is a steward. Nothing belongs to you. You are a supervisor. If you supervise wrong you will not be graduated. Your body was given to you to be used for the Purpose. Your heart was given to you to use for the Purpose. Non-essentials waste your time, energy, money, and your soul. This is a very very heavy idea. Who can always live in the most essential--- That is our challenge — that year after year we minimize non-essentials and increase the labor for the most essential.

As a child, you had lots of toys. What happened to those toys? Why are you not carrying those toys now in your pockets? You outgrew them. It was one phase. But how are your going to outgrow now the level of consciousness that you have, the attitudes you have, the crystallizations you have? How are you going to outgrow them? That is the path. Every time you outgrow yourself, transcend yourself, you build your own path and increase the beauty and radiation of your soul.

Every time you lose yourself in non-essentials, you become a non-essential. But the human mind is cemented to such a degree that these ideas need maybe another thousand years to be welcomed. Some houses have entry rooms where you leave your jacket when you are visiting. It is just like our mind. Our mind has that room. We take off our shoes and say how nice it is but we do not enter the real house. The real house is entered when you start really understanding what we are talking about. But you will say, "On the other hand." When you start saying, "On the other hand," you are lost already because you will be on the other hand.

Unconditional understanding, unconditional dedication to the most essential is very important. We say, "What is the nearest space from here to there?" You will say it is a straight line. Of course, it is a straight line. If you go zigzag it takes too long. To live a straight line is to dedicate yourself to the most essential, whatever it is for you. No one can tell you what the most essential is. You find it. Sometimes our soul is so blocked that it has a skin one inch thick. Nothing can penetrate that skin. You think, "What are you talking about? It does not make sense." Of course, it will not make sense because there is no sense to receive the sense. You must have a sense to *smell* it. Here you are walking in the rotten street and saying, "There is nothing smelling bad here." Your nose is crooked and you cannot smell. When you go to the store you do not buy every kind of trash, but you try to find something which is not trash. You buy something which is good. You go to the shoemakers and you buy the shoes you want. These are the first and second steps of understanding what is the most essentials.

Of course, the most essential concerns go to your thinking, feelings, and reactions. You have five hundred people saying one thing and five hundred people saying something else. What is your attitude? Are you with the most essentials or a pendulum swinging back and forth? The practice of the most essential or pursuit of the most essential eventually creates a state of consciousness within you which is like a tower of stability. You must try to be stable mentally but, if you cannot be mentally stable, all you are doing is creating instability.

How can you create stability within your mind, within your soul, within your being? You can do it by the exercise of identifying yourself with the most essential thoughts, feelings, attitudes, actions. Then you create stability within you. But if you are today here, tomorrow there with your emotions, mind, and activities, that diamond of stability cannot be created in your consciousness. This is just like saying that if you are dating two hundred people, you lose your stability. Stability is to narrow them down to one. You have millions of ideas. Squeeze them, synthesize them into one, the most essential.

For example, someone says, "You are going to be taken to the moon because our world is in danger. A special aircraft will be sent for your use, but you can take only ten kilos with you." What are you going to take? One day a man surprised me by asking, "If you were to go to the moon today, what would you take with you?" I said, "I will take M.M. books." "Only one book," he said. "I will take *Infinity*.[1] I do not want anything else." This is an exercise for you to think about yourself. How are you going to deal with your life, with your wife, with your husband? Are you going to bring, every day, non-essential trash to discuss and debate with him or her, or are you going to stay on the platform of the most essential?

You can lose or kill your soul by not nourishing your soul. How can you nourish your soul? First, you can live for the

1. *Infinity, I & II*, published by the Agni Yoga Society.

most essential, meditating to find out if the most essential is what you want. Fix it, check it, see it, and then by striving, release the potentials that are hidden within you. That is how you can nourish your soul. The most essential nourishes the soul because they it does not waste the soul. Today, there are fifty parties. Which one do you want to go to? You have five hundred dollars. Where are you going to spend it? You have one life. How are you going to spend this life, where, how? You have one soldier. Where are you going to use that one soldier? He must be used for the most essential.

Second, check it through meditation. What are you checking? You are checking to see if that most essential is the one you want. Yes, it is. Are you ready for it? What do you need to exercise it, practice it, cultivate it, and use it in your life? A lady said, "I am not going to come to your lectures anymore because you say too much." I wish you would come and that time will be the most beautiful.

Third, there is striving to bring the treasures out which are hidden within you. Why are you a great treasure? It is because God is within you; you are part of that Almighty Power, whatever It is. You are a seed of an oak tree. That acorn must start being an oak. You are going to check. Yesterday I was watching a film. They were checking monkeys, how they grow, their eyes and ears, to see if everything is natural, proportionate, beautiful? Yes. But you never check your inner monkey to see how he is growing. How is your monkey growing? What kind of monkey are you? Monkeys now are more precious than humans. For five monkeys we are spending five billion dollars. How much are you spending for your perfection, finding the treasures within you?

One day a girl came and asked me to perform her marriage. I said, "Of course." The girl said, "I have a confidential thing to tell you. We do not have money." "That is alright. My service is for you. Come anytime and I will perform the marriage ceremony." Two hundred people also came with them and then they invited me to their party. We all went to the party and they sat me at the head table. Every table had whiskey on it. I blessed the table and then said, "Lady, good-bye." "Where are you going?" " It is impossible. I must go. I cannot sit at a table which is surrounded by hypocrites. You cannot give twenty dollars to the Group and here you have a thousand dollars' worth of whiskey. Shame on you."

Where are you spending your money? Is it the most essential to take the blessings of your Father or to drink and get intoxicated? How can we find the most essential? That is why we emphasize discrimination, discrimination, discrimination. But discrimination is translated politically ; they think we are discriminating between races and colors and so on. Discrimination means intelligent choice between the real and the unreal. When you start discriminating, observing, and meditating, you will find that these three things that nourish your soul will eventually be tools in your hands.

The first is to find the most essential, the second is meditation, and the third is striving to bring the treasures out which are hidden within you. Whenever you have an argument with somebody or you have difficulties, stop one minute and say, "I have a chance to go to my brain, to my storage, and bring the most awful things out or the most beautiful things out." Which do you want? Either you open your mouth and bring the sewerage out or you try to bring the beauty out, the Divine Essentials which are in your soul.

You kill your soul by falling into traps. There are traps of treason, cheating, deception, and hypocrisy. These are traps. Once you tell a lie you are trapped, because you want to tell another ten lies to release yourself. When you cannot release yourself you speak more, and then you are trapped within your own network. If you beat a man you are trapped because to prevent him from beating you, you will be beat him.. His friends will come and you beat them and they will beat you. You are trapped. You are in the fight.

How to let your soul survive? As much as possible do not trap yourself because every trap is laid there to kill you. The traps are within us: deception, hypocrisy, cheating people for our own sake, manipulating them, exploiting them with beautiful idealistic expressions. "I am going to kill you because it is God's glory." Do not cheat people. Do not be a hypocrite of many faces so that nobody can see the real face. It is better to live simply and sincerely and openly so that you enjoy the life which is given to you. Why do you want to complicate it? The straight path is the path of total sincerity.

You kill your soul by serving your separativeness, ego, greed, vanity, and illusions. As long as you are serving your glamors, your soul is dying. If you are serving your illusions, vanities, ego, separatism, your soul is dying. How to tell these things to humanity? We do not really understand the laws of the Universe. The laws of the Universe are to live a life which is egoless there is no vanity in your life, there is no cheating yourself. To cheat yourself means that you have an ego within you. Do not cheat yourself.

There is a sin which you can never erase and that is cheating yourself. Knowing the truth you cheat yourself. If you stand in the light, stay there. Do not stay in the light and serve darkness. If you are in darkness, stay in darkness so that we see you. If you are in the light, stay in the light and die for the light.

Greed is devastating the world. Your greed devastates your own personal life. You go to the prisons and eighty percent of the prisoners say they are the victims of their greed. A man in high position was put in prison because he stole ten million dollars. A man went to a store and stole beer and other groceries. Why are they doing that? Greed.

The other day a girl was traveling. She saw three people sitting on the hood of a car looking sad. The girl went over to them and asked, "What is the matter?" "We do not have money for gas." She gave them fifty dollars. That is the American spirit. Stay in that spirit because that will nourish your soul. People think that greed is the evidence of poverty. It is not. Greed is a sickness. It a cancer of the mind. Cancer of the mind expresses itself as greed. If you go and investigate people who have brain tumors, you will see that they lived a greedy life. It is a mental disease.

By not being a responsible human being you kill your soul. What does this mean? By losing your purpose of life you lose your soul.

Of course others can kill your soul by misleading you into those activities which waste your time, energy, and life. They make you waste your life, and lose your purpose of life.

Q&A

Question: Sometimes during the day you are really obnoxious and really angry, but later you realize it and are so ashamed. How can you be more aware?

Answer: That is why there is some great literature available, such as Dante's writings, *Bhagavad Gita, Upanishads*, and other writings in which they explain that our daily life is a war. We must be very careful which side is winning within us: darkness or light, love or hatred, justice or injustice. It is a battle.

If you read the first chapter of the *Bhagavad Gita*, Krishna came to Arjuna and said, "There are two sides, this side and that side. You are going to fight." Arjuna came and saw that they were his family. They were his teachers and friends. "I do not want to fight against them." Arjuna fell down into the carriage with deep depression. Krishna said, "You are going to fight within you to find out who your enemy is, what your enemy is. Can you find it?"

Go one day and sit on a rock and ask, "Which thought is the enemy within me; which attitude is an enemy within me? Which action do I not approve of but I do it anyhow?" If you start this introspection, you can find out what is going on within you. You are on the path, but if you cannot find which is your friend inside, which is your enemy inside, you are an automaton. You are used by the winds of the life. You do not have a private existence. You are existing for any influence that makes you live according to its interests. You do not have your life. You do not have the most essential. You are pushed to think, to feel the way that it wants. That is the best way to lose yourself.

> ***Question:*** *When you say "to think and to feel" are you saying that these characteristics like vanity, ego, and separatism can be found in all three of the bodies?*

Answer: The better way to present this is not to think of vanity, ego, separatism, hatred, jealousy. Do not take them as names. See in your life what you are doing which is not for the best interest and you find it out. Do not call it cheating, but speak and then you find that people are confused. Then say, "I am doing something wrong." Correct yourself. Do not believe the words and sentences. You check your life and say, "What am I doing that is wrong?"

In my teaching I do not say this is wrong, this is right. You do anything you want. You find out what is wrong and what is right because if I tell you something is right, it might be wrong for you. And if I say something is wrong for you, maybe it is right for you. Why to create karma? You find it out. That is what discipleship is.

I once told my Teacher I had read so many books on discipleship and heard so many things and asked him to tell me something that I will never forget. He said, "Come here. See that mirror. Look at yourself. That is discipleship." Find a way really to see yourself, and if you cannot find a way to see yourself you are blind. See yourself and what you are, really see physically, emotionally, mentally. When you really see yourself it is a very psychological process. When you seeing yourself, you start destroying the masks in whicl are hidden. You were seeing your masks, pretensions, ii tions, self-deceptions. This is good for you, good for income, for your health, for your social attitudes and c tions, healthy for your soul. That is discipleship — ı yourself. Instead of saying to a man, "You have dirt on face," it is better to say, "Do you mind looking in the mirroı for one minute?" "No, I do not mind." Well, you will mind after seeing yourself.

Sometimes our life is like this. I was once swimming in the river in Kern County when the dam was opened and the rush of water came and took me with it. I enjoyed the first few minutes, but then I started to worry about where I was going. Another minute later I panicked and searched for a branch to hang on to. Eventually I saw a big rock and was afraid if I hit the rock I would be finished. Instead, I jumped on the rock and sat there. We are driven by these tides. You do not have time to think, to face yourself, because you are in the tide. Security comes when you find a rock to get out of the tide. That rock is your spiritual reality within you. That was a great experience in my life, trying to get out of that current.

That is what it is when Buddha speaks about voidness. Do not be full of old trash. Find one minute of serenity and voidness. Thank God for peace and beauty. Now you can think. As long as you are in the current, you do not have the time and opportunity to think, and this current can be a pleasant and an awful current. Go to the bars. People are drinking, doping, and dancing. They are so happy. They are in the current. They are in pleasant currents, but pleasant currents are going to take them and dump them to the universe.

I read in the Ageless Wisdom, "The explosion of a human soul in space contaminates millions of miles." It is something which must not happen, but it happens. Do not kill your soul. Nourish it, be beautiful, live for Light, Love, and Beauty.

Question: What is the "near death" experience?

Answer: Near-death experience is the moment when the human soul is between the etheric body and the astral body. At that moment you are very sensitive. The same thing occurs when you are entering sleep, or when you are awakening from sleep. M.M. says that these two periods are the times in which you can have valuable psychic experiences. This occurs because you are linking with the astral world and being linked with the etheric body, you can register and record the experiences that are happening on the astral or mental planes.

The same phenomenon occurs when you are sleeping or awakening. It is the same mechanism. Many great visions and experiences occur just at those moments.

But if you have withdrawn from the etheric brain and you enter into the astral plane, you do not *register* new experiences.

Let us say that you are going to the astral plane. As long as you are in both — the etheric brain and the astral/mental planes — you are receiving experiences from the astral/mental planes and registering them in the etheric brain. But if you are in the astral/mental planes without also being connected with your etheric brain, there is no registration. In such a case, you are in deep sleep. Or, if you are in the etheric brain and not connected to the astral/mental bodies, you are in the physical body. You register events in the subtle planes when your Antahkarana is built.

The etheric/physical body has an etheric brain and a physical brain. Let us say that you are in these two bodies. In the meantime you are extended to the astral/mental planes through your Antahkarana. All of your experiences are registered in the etheric brain, then in your physical brain. In a state of ecstasy or in a *conscious* trance state, you receive and register higher impressions because you have built a bridge between the two levels. This is the period when you register things from subjective levels. You can learn to come into such a state when you do real meditation. Real meditation is to be in the etheric/physical and the subjective levels simultaneously.

The human soul is anchored in the pineal gland, but his consciousness can identify itself with any center. Usually our consciousness is identified with our sex center, then solar plexus, then heart, then throat center.

Each progress corresponds to one of the levels of the mental plane. When your consciousness works toward the heart center, you are in the fourth level of the mind. From there, from the mental unit, you will build the *bridge* toward the mental permanent atom. It is after this bridge is built that you experience continuity of consciousness.

Question: *How does this relate to imagination?*

Answer: Imagination is totally different. Imagination is when you are in the astral body, using the astral body and imagining and building astral forms. You are not experiencing anything; you are building forms. Imagination is to take astral plane substance and formulate it into the shapes of your desires, wishes, dreams, and hallucinations. Imagination has *nothing* to do with the registration just previously mentioned.

Question: *I heard that the human soul is anchored in the* heart. *What heart is that?*

Answer: The heart referred to is the Chalice in the second level of the mental body. When the Chalice is dissipated during the Fourth Initiation, the human soul moves into the heart center in the thousand petaled Lotus.

The anchorage or the contact point of the human soul with the physical plane is the pineal gland. But the consciousness of the human soul can identify itself with a lower center and fool itself. The consciousness can also identify with higher centers and expand the awareness of the soul. Also, the soul can leave the mental plane and wander millions of miles away, having the anchorage in the pineal gland.

Question: *What is the auric body?*

Answer: The advanced or pure souls enter into a long lasting state of consciousness which in the Ageless Wisdom is called *devachan.* It is in this state that all the past is forgotten and beauty and peace and bliss are experienced.

Those who work and live for beauty, peace, and bliss are those who had the experience in the *devachanic* state, and hence they want to bring beauty, peace, and bliss to earth in all their activities.

In *The Secret Doctrine* we read about a body that plays an important role for those who enter into *devachanic* consciousness.

The Auric Body"... at death... assimilates the essence of Buddhi and Manas and becomes the vehicle of these spiritual principles, *which are not objective*, and then, with the full radiation of Atma upon it ascends as Manas-Taijasi into the devachanic state....It is the sutratma, the silver 'thread' which 'incarnates' from the beginning of Manvantara to the end, stringing upon itself the pearls of human existence, in other words, the spiritual aroma of every personality it *follows* through the pilgrimage of life. It is also the material from which the adept forms his Astral Bodies from the Augoeides and the Mayavid Rupa downwards...."[2] *Taijasi* means originating from light.

2. H.P. Blavatsky, *The Secret Doctrine,* Vol. III, p. 446.

12

How Others Can Kill Your Soul

We will now discuss how we kill other souls or how other people kill our soul.

The soul is the light that you travel by. If you do not have that light, you are in darkness. The soul is the light that leads you to other worlds. When your body passes away, it is the light of the soul that guides you in higher dimensions. It is with the soul that you understand the value of other people. You appreciate them. It is the soul that makes you a human being. And if your soul is killed, you do not exist because *you* are your own soul.

I am going to explain what "killing" means. There are five points that will make you understand the meaning of killing:

1. If you kill the souls of other people, you make them insensitive to spiritual values. They become insensitive. They are doped. Spiritual values do not exist for them. So it means their soul is killed or in the process of decay.

2. The second way is making them blind to their future spiritual goals. That is a sign that the soul is dying.

3. Being a disintegrating individuality means to die as a soul. It is interesting to talk to people and watch them.

Their individuality is disintegrating. Some of them do not have individuality. They are confused. Even they do not know what they are. They have millions of images in their minds. They think — "This image is mine. No, this image is me. That image may be what I am now." But they do not have a central image in which they can put their faith and use it as their foundation. These kinds of people we call confused people.

When you use the word "confusion" in its general meaning, it does not have a deep meaning. But in higher levels confusion means a devastating state of beingness — devastating — because confusion means you do not have direction, you do not know who you are, you do not even know that you exist. You are lost in the space. When you are lost, it means you are confused. Confusion is the first step toward suicide.

4. Killing in others the sense of direction and responsibility is killing the souls of other people.

5. The next method is killing the instinctive resistance to evil in other people. That is so subtle. You can see these things working in your radio, television, newspapers, everywhere. They kill the resistance in you to stand against evil. When this instinctual resistance is killed, your soul is decayed.

For a man to kill his own soul is a great crime, but not greater than the crime of killing another's soul. When you kill the soul of another person, all that is related to that person is killed, slowly killed along with that killed soul. When your soul dies, you become a disintegrating personality.

Master Morya says that soulless people are just dead animals. Their radiated particles cause other people to disintegrate. It is a very serious matter but unfortunately people never talk about these things.

Now, let us talk about how we can kill or other people can kill our own souls. We must be so careful that we do not tolerate people to kill our souls, and we must be very careful that we do not kill other souls.

1. The first way is by leading them into a spirit of hatred, revenge, self-deceit, and separativeness. This is how you can kill the souls of other people, and this is going on everywhere in legal and professional ways. You must not lead people into the spirit of hatred, revenge, self-deceit, and separativeness.

2. You kill the souls of other people by sidetracking their interests and attention from the purpose of life and keeping them busy with their non-essentials. You keep them so busy putting their nose into the trash that they do not have a chance to look up. These are very serious. I wish some of you would sit down and write a book for each one of these points. Each one can be a book. It is so revealing to know these things.

If you sidetrack people, pull their attention away from the purpose of life and keep them busy with non-essentials, you will start killing their souls. You may hear, "Why do you want to go to a university? Become some human being who makes money. Why are you interested in Higher Worlds and spiritual realities and God? They do not pay you anything for that. Just go and carry the rubbish and make lots of money."

"Why be righteous because righteousness never brings you money? Be unrighteous. Deceive people instead of speaking the truth." That is how they keep you occupied with the trash. Once you are occupied with the trash, karma gets you and you do not have a chance to run away from that circuit. You run after your tail continuously, and you do not have a chance to stop one minute and think about the purpose of your life. That is what the world is doing for us — promising big jobs, big positions, millions of dollars. You are trapped. You do not know how beautifully you are trapped.

That is why Christ said something so important. It was not religion He was talking about. "First of all search for the Kingdom of God," and the Kingdom of God is nothing else but your soul. Find your soul. In fact do not just find your soul. Be your soul. Make it a reality that exists because the soul is the source of all virtues and values and the creative source of all beauty, if you find it.

3. By inflaming people's ego, vanity, and greed, you kill their souls. Do people do these things? Of course! University level! All advertisements are to increase your greed. Greed, greed — you have one acre. It is not enough. Get another ten acres, millions of acres. "You are so beautiful, you are the greatest human being, and he is a trash." You flatter each other, put ego in them and vanity. When the ego and vanity and greed increase, first of all, they eat your soul. Your soul is eaten. If there is an artist here, he can portray greed — big nose and teeth. Vanity is something else, a

viper. Ego is a big dungeon and here man is caught in it. He does not have a chance to think about his soul.

Every time we try to kill the souls of other people we engage ourselves in worse and worse karma. Karma is another dungeon that does not give us time to breathe. For example, you are caught in a court case. You run day and night, worry day and night, pay day and night, and you say, "When am I going to get rid of it?" You get rid of one case and ten cases open. That is what the karma is. That is very bad.

4. By training people how to kill, how to cheat, how to manipulate, how to exploit we kill their souls. Do we teach killing? Of course. All over the world crime is 90% increasing. Why? Because we have good teachers, teaching us how to kill scientifically, legally, professionally, philosophically, psychologically, biologically. I am not kidding you. Mentally, they are killing the souls by training people how to kill, how to cheat. Cheating is like a knife hitting the other soul. Of course, you are not killing it immediately, but already it is wounded. Ten times more and you will bury it. This is what we do to our children. I am skipping more dangerous things here. Yes, I am serious.

5. By being an example of ugliness, unrighteousness, hatred, revenge, and deceit, you kill the souls of your children and those with whom you are related. Can you run away from them? You cannot. But why be an example of ugliness? You see a movie, and an actor is playing a role of ugliness. Millions of people are contaminated by it. And a little voice says, "You contaminated them." Our amusements

are making people irresponsible for the well being of other human beings. They are manipulating our feelings and thinking. How bad is it to make people irresponsible for the well being of other people? "Who cares? They are black, they are yellow, they are green, they are Indian, they are this, they are that. They are no good. Why are they no good? They are not like us. That is the reason."

Really? To be like you is to be really good? That is standard thinking. If you are from here, that is your standard. You can force it. You can even shut their eyes by putting some dollars there. That is happening every day.

This subject is so beautiful. This will save you. There is no intention to hurt your feelings. If you eliminate these things, we will become happy, healthy, prosperous, peaceful, creative, beautiful because the source of your beauty, creativity, health, happiness is your soul, a healthy soul. Some people do not have a healthy psyche, a healthy soul. They are sick.

What do you call a man who is killing hundreds of people and enjoying it? He is sick. Or he has no soul at all.

6. Making other people abandon their principles of purity and beauty kills their soul and ours. I saw a film four or five years ago. A prostitute was teaching three little girls how to be prostitutes. One of the girls said, "I do not like it." "Oh," the prostitute said, "that is in your mind. That is your feeling. Something is wrong with you. You are not normal. You are abnormal. If you would be normal you must be a prostitute." And the girl said, "Yea, all right." She killed it.

You kill it when you say, "What's wrong with taking a little drink." You say, "Sip a little alcohol," as if he is going to be a "cowboy" if he drinks. You say, "A little more. How nice you are doing." He goes to a party, drinks a little more, and then he kills somebody. You killed his soul.

Where are you leading that boy? You are beautiful people, but you do not know what is happening in other homes, in the slums, in big cities. Children are left there. There is no father or mother. They are like dogs wandering everywhere.

In many cities there are hundreds of little children, four and five years old, just like dogs, going from one trash can to another to find a little something to eat.

Look where we are leading our children. This is happening now in many places in the world because some people want to be victorious, because some people are not sane, because there are dictatorships and totalitarianism. That is what is happening all over the world. It is difficult. Maybe some of you will be surprised.

7. You kill people's souls when you encourage them to occupy themselves with necromancy and mediumship. Necromancy is speaking with dead souls. You are hooking them to something that will destroy their life. I saw this. I was in Indianapolis. I saw three pretty girls walking back and forth. I said, "Wow, what pretty girls they are." I asked them, "What do you want?" They said, "We are looking for our teacher. He is not here." I asked, "What is he going to teach you?" They said, "Well, we are sitting and communicating with the dead." I said, "Go home. He will kill your soul.

Really." I said, "it is so dangerous. Even in the Bible and in other places they told us not to do such kinds of things." They said that if you see any people occupied with dead people, stone them and kill them. And, here, everybody is doing these kind of things. It is legal now.

Are you afraid? Don't be afraid. I am going to say good things soon, but this is so important to know. If you know the dangers, you will be a little awake and people will not try to kill your soul. Look at how beautiful the next one is.

8. In taking away people's freedom and joy, you kill their soul. But you do it so technically that they do not feel that their freedom is gone or their joy is gone. Professionally and scientifically you know what to do.

But karma is observing you. The big eye is seeing what you are doing. Taking the joys of other people kills their soul. Let them enjoy their life. Taking the freedom of other people means to destroy the plan of God that was put in that man. He is going to be a lily; he is going to be a rose; he is going to be a draftsman. "No, no, no," you say, "you are going to be a tomato." Here you are working against the will of the Almighty Presence. Do not take the freedom of other people nor their joy. Let them enjoy the life.

When you see people undermining your freedom and joy, be careful because it is the start of killing your soul. We learned these things in monasteries, not from the books. Did you read any book about this? No, because that is part of the conspiracy. "Why write about these things? Join the party."

9. By imparting false information to people, you kill the light of their soul. They can no longer think right be-

cause you are giving wrong information. Do not be afraid of right information, but be afraid when people say wrong things, false things.

You stole one chicken. Ok, they say you stole two thousand chickens. "Wow! Let's cut his hand off." That is false information! In the Bible we read that Satan is called the false informer, the cheater. Isn't that interesting. He cheats people. He deceives people. So Satan's prime purpose is to kill your soul. Satan is a dark force. It exists. I saw it. Believe me. But I will tell that story another day. I came face to face. I do not believe books if they are not written by people who are experienced.

Try never to give false information. Slander, malice, and treason are all parts of false information based on self-interest, hatred, malice, jealousy, this or that.

You can be a friend to somebody and he will speak so highly about you. But once you step on his tail, he will give radio messages to everybody that you are the worst man ever created. Do not give false information because you kill the lights of the people and prevent them from seeing the reality. Whenever people prevent you from seeing reality, they are killing your soul. Do you see that? This is not a sermon.

10. By preventing other people from building a relationship with the Higher Worlds, you kill their soul because you make them earthbound. "Whatever exists is in this world. There is nothing else." Kruschev said once that we sent jets and airplanes but we did not send anything to heaven in the sky, as if heaven is a location. That stupid man did not know that heaven is a state of consciousness. And that state of con-

sciousness can be in an atom, in the people you know. A state of consciousness is not a location. He was fooling his people.

I saw many children who want to go, for example, to church. They want to go to groups and listen to them. They want to go and read the Teaching. They want to do meditation. But father comes and says, "What are you doing?" "I am meditating." "Meditating? You are crazy! Stop it." By saying these things you are killing the soul of that person. Let them be free.

There was a woman who was killing her daughter by preventing her from being a ballerina. She wants to dance day and night and become a ballerina. Her mother wouldn't let her, so she became a prostitute and criminal. Why did you do that? Who is going to pay for that?

Do not kill the souls of people.

11. By teaching them to be materialistic, totalitarian, and self-interested, you kill their soul for centuries. That is what Communism did. That is what Fascism, Nazism did. That is what others are doing. I am afraid to give names. Don't teach totalitarianism. All these criminals are taught totalitarianism, self-interest, and materialism. You see that a man has a million dollars. He engages in treason and gives all your nation's secrets to other nations. Self-interest. It is so he can get a little more money? His soul is killed. Matter killed him. That is why that man came to Jesus and said, "Master, can you teach me how to go to heaven." He thought Jesus could put up a ladder and make him to climb. "My son," He said, "you must keep the commandments." "Oh, I

did that." If some man says that he did, that is a big lie and also a sign it is a big lie. Who are you to do that? But if you can say, "I am trying," I will accept that.

So Jesus says to "sell everything that you have and follow me." The man started to cry and went away, and Jesus said that this kind of person cannot enter into the Kingdom of Heaven for they are attached to self-interest, materialism, totalitarianism. Totalitarianism means to be attached to whatever you have and be the king of what you have.

12. Killing in the minds of the people the spirit of admiration for higher values kills the soul. "Mozart, he was insane. Dostoyevsky, stupid. Lincoln, he was a trash. Shubert, mongoloid." Do you understand what you are doing? What to believe then if you are taking everything that I worship? How am I going to strive anymore? You cut the source of my aspiration, my striving, my progress. You are saying my God is no good, Christ is no good, this is no good. Why do you do that? Give something to people to worship because in worshipping you become bigger than you are. Do you understand that? Do you understand how beautiful that is? Do not take the level of other people and destroy them. She likes Lincoln and Lincoln is like a God for her. How wonderful! Let her have it because that image will pull her toward the consciousness of Lincoln. Do not kill the values, the admiration. Admiration is a great sense that I did not find discussed in any book. Pitiful. Eighteen million years people are living and they did not write any book about admiration, about what admiration is.

What is admiration? It is an instinct to see beauty and to identify with beauty. That is admiration. People do not have admiration if they do not say, "Wow, what a beautiful thing is this!"

13. An unforgiving attitude kills the soul. Such an attitude like a termite destroys the foundations of the souls of others. "Well, you hit my nose fifteen years ago." Still you are sitting and talking about how he hit you nose. Can you forgive? "If I forgive you will do it again." That is the reason behind it.

14. Another way is with a continuous current of hatred and revenge directed toward individuals and groups. Such an attitude cuts their life thread and destroys their soul continuously. That is why my Dad once said, "Try not to make people hate you." I was not always able to do what he said. "But," he said, "Be honest." I said, "Daddy, you are saying something that is impossible!" "Yes," he said, "But when impossible things are made possible, you take initiation." Then I said, "All right. I will try." When millions of people are hating you, it is very hard not to go to hell.

15. Not feeding the soul according to its age kills the soul. When this baby needs baby food, you are feeding him *Cosmic Fire, Secret Doctrine*. You are saying, "Sit down and do ten hours of meditation." What are you doing? He does not know yet where his nose is, and you are talking about the stars. You are killing him. See how we kill people with good intentions? That is why you must be careful about what you are saying. This is a very serious thing which needs one hour to discuss.

16. Wasting our time, energy, and money to feed our pleasures, our pleasure-seeking personality and its stupidity will kill our soul.

17. By losing chances to do sacrificial service or by failing to take responsibilities the soul is killed. That man and woman are ready to sacrifice, to dedicate their lives. There is a chance and you prevent it. You do not give a chance to them. You kill their souls.

Signs of Living Souls

What are the signs of living souls? There are six signs. They are so beautiful. Later think about them, talk about them in detail.

Industriousness is a sign that your soul is alive. Some ladies and some gentlemen are just like potatoes. They sit there and they roll a little. Come on, do something. Clean your house. Go work in the garden. Do something physically, emotionally, mentally, spiritually — something. When you start doing something diligently, industriously, then that is a sign that your soul is alive.

Solemnity. Every time you escape from solemnity you are killing your soul. Solemnity is persistence in striving toward your goal. If you are doing things that are taking you away from your goal, you are not a solemn person. Solemnity comes from Latin. *Sole* means one direction. Solemnity is to engage yourself in one direction. But that direction is a goal, is a purpose in your life. When you do things against your own predestined goal, you are fooling around. And those who fool around are not solemn people. Hierarchy takes from them the responsibility that They were going to give them.

Creativity is a sign of aliveness, of joy, and of increasing interest in the future labor, in the labor of the future. How nice it is when people ask, "What will our planet be in 200 years if pollution like this increases?" Everywhere the tanks and gases are burning. If pesticides and insecticides are increasing, what will be the future of our planet? These are alive people because they think of their future children. This includes a lot of people. Also, they think about themselves in future incarnations.

Inclusiveness is a sign that your soul is alive.

Sincerity is a sign of soul because every time you become a hypocrite, you are something else than what you are. You create a short circuit within you, within your psychic system. This is so beautiful. Put it in your "computer."

Stability is another sign. Are you stable?

These signs are so beautiful to think about. I do not know when I will have a chance to speak again about these things.

Q&A

Question: How do you revive the soul?

Answer: I think to bring back your soul you must remember what wrong you did and you must try to have a great, great aspiration and desire to repair the damage that you did. Then you can start thinking about higher values with utmost sincerity and feed the soul with the Teaching. The Teaching feeds your soul. Everything that is beautiful and righteous and good and joyful and free feeds your soul. You tell people to go and take some vitamins, but I suggest you take vitamins of Beauty, Goodness, Truth, Joy, Freedom, Striving, Gratitude, and Solemnity. These are pills, pills for your soul. Honesty, nobility are higher vitamins that you cannot find in the herb stores. "But I don't need **these** vitamins. What else can I do for my body?" Well, we say that when the soul dies, your whole body degenerates. That is why the real Chinese medicine, the real Tibetan or Indian medicine was to feed your soul first. Any time you are sick, they do not look at your body. They say that sickness is the result of the sickness of your soul. Your soul became sick somewhere in some part, and that is why your body is sick. I started to believe that because when I get sick, I did something wrong.

> *Question: Are you referring only to the developing human soul?*

Answer: Yes, only that. That is a big story because we talk about whether a man has a soul or not. Average Buddhists say that man has no soul because they have degenerated from the real Teaching. They do not know what they are saying.

Question: If one is aware of some of the psychic attacks or some unforgiveness or hatred toward you, what can you do?

Answer: Immediately change your thoughtform and send positive thoughtforms. For example, there was a girl who was increasing her jealousy. I was watching how jealousy went from one person to two, three persons, from three persons to ten persons and she started to be jealous about this, about that. I said, "Wow, gangrene entered into her soul." I called her and said that there was one salvation for her. "What?" I said, "Send love and gratitude to everybody that you are jealous of." She said, "There are so many I cannot tell you, Torkom." She is degenerating now. And some people like to relate to degenerated people.

Question: What is the relationship between curing the heart and curing the soul?

Answer: Same thing. They are just two eyes. You kill one eye, then you kill the next one. I wrote a book about the heart. You should read it.

Question: If you feel that you are being attacked, what should you do?

Answer: It does not matter. That is what I am saying. I am answering wholesale. Whether you are attacking or others are attacking, create good thoughtforms. Read Master Morya. What does He say? "The greatest shield is a pure thought," which means if you do not have pure thoughts, you do not have a shield. And if you do not have a shield, you are under attack. The implications are so big.

Question: There are lots of people who are trying to kill the souls on this planet. Can the soul of the planet be killed?

Answer: Yes. The soul of the moon was killed in a certain degree. Yes, as above, so below. Whatever happens here can happen above. When you have had some experiences, you will see that it is the same world — higher and higher and higher. Actually, it is an echo. Sometimes things happen here because of what is happening there. But shield yourself and the cells in the body will be healthy cells. Try to be healthy cells in the body of humanity.

Question: Is the Solar Angel intervening?

Answer: No. As the Teacher says, read and do whatever you want. They are totally disinterested. But They give warnings cyclically. Unfortunately our ears become so dull that we cannot hear, but we must hear it!

13

Lost Souls

Lost souls are discussed in the Teaching of the Great Ones. These souls are thrown out from the planet or out of the solar system, and all their vehicles melt away into the ocean of chaotic forces in space.

In some cases the Spark still exists but in total unconsciousness. It waits for another Manvantara when a new chance will be given to it to start again the long path of evolution.

There are souls and Sparks who are almost ready for extinction, but some past sacrifice or good deed saves them and gives them the chance to continue their evolution. Conscious sacrifice and selfless service are factors that illuminate our path of ascent and protect us from falling into the path of dissolution.

Identity is formed through a long series of lives of striving and labor. It is identity that must be saved from dissolution. Through the experiences of life, identity builds up and continuously recreates old bodies and builds new ones. But the extinction of identity is the greatest calamity that can happen to a person.

Identity is the realization of Self, an increasing awareness of One Self. It is the true Individuality that exists within the Greater Self. This Individuality is brought into existence through the process of unfoldment of the Monad, the Spark, and through the help of the Inner Guide — like a pearl forming in an oyster.

This Individuality can lose Its communication, Its awareness of Itself, lose all Its vehicles and fall into the ocean of space without identity.

Of course, man in his essence is a Monad. But this does not mean that a Monad does not dissolve. Once man is stripped of his identity, he slowly returns to the ocean of space, like a bubble that bursts in the ocean.

What is the difference between an identity that is lost in the ocean and one that reaches the ocean through age-long striving and becomes one with the ocean? The answer is that the first one loses all consciousness and awareness. The second one keeps his awareness and realizes himself in the Self-conscious Ocean.

The human soul is a focus of individualized fire, like a diamond, which cycle after cycle uses new bodies to come in contact with physical, emotional, and mental realms. As long as this human soul exists, the incarnations become possible. Once the human soul is dissipated or lost for certain reasons, the bodies cannot come into incarnation and they dissolve in corresponding spheres, carrying with them their bad influence.

Why does this dissipation or annihilation of the human soul occur?

The Ageless Wisdom says that the Solar Angel leaves the person because of his inhuman, destructive actions, actions that break the law of love, unity, and synthesis. After the Solar Angel leaves the person, the destructive fires of the Universe rush toward the human soul, the electrical, fiery forces, and eventually cause disintegration in it. Eventually the human soul dissolves like a flame that is blown out by the wind.

If this happens while in a physical body, the body lives for a while, then passes away, sometimes in accidents, suicides, or in explosions. The person is no more. The work of ages to create the individualization is wasted. But still his records in Akasha remain and are available for those who study such cases.

Ancients say that one must keep the flame always lit. The fire of Zoroaster was the symbol of the human soul. This fire must be kept alive forever, without interruption. The fuel of this fire is

- Good thoughts
- Pure thoughts
- Good words
- Pure words
- Good actions
- Pure actions

This is how the flame in the heart is kept burning. The soul is nourished by the fuel of pure thoughts, words, and actions.

Pure thoughts, pure words, and pure actions are sparks of electrical fire which nourish the human soul. The human soul becomes more focused and dynamic in relation to his bodies as he is nourished by these sparks of fire.

These sparks of fire are radiations of the fire of the human soul. The human soul unfolds and expands his field of radiation as he emanates the currents of fire which manifest as pure thoughts, as pure words, and as pure actions.

It is through such fiery sparks that the continuity of existence of the soul is secured.

The human soul must reach a certain stage of density to turn into a diamond that does not disintegrate under certain antagonistic currents.

Our thoughts, words, and deeds live for a long period of time. If they are charged by purity, they transmit to space the benevolent fires of the human soul.

But if they are not charged by the fiery currents of the soul, they suck the energies of the human soul in order to survive and, in the meantime, cause disintegration to the human soul.

A man is a fruit on the tree of life. Many fruits fall, disintegrate, and disappear. But the fruit that has a healthy core, a fiery core that contains regenerative and creative currents of fire, it perpetuates its life, becomes a new tree and produces many fruits.

Every human soul during the fruition must reach to the state of individualization and develop continuity of consciousness. Individualization is a stage of consciousness in which the core of the fruit, the human soul, feels adequate to have *his independent life,* a stage of consciousness in which he becomes aware that his life was given by the tree, and the awareness that he too can be a tree.

The tree symbolizes the Life-current in the Universe, the ray of life in every form, in human form. The human soul is a fruit on this Life-current. It is an individualized Life-current with all the innate capabilities to cooperate with the creativity of that Life-current.

If the fruit does not reach maturity on the Life-current on the tree, it eventually dries out and disintegrates in the soil. But if the fruit reaches maturity with self-induced striving and conscious discipline, it can start its own "independent" life, burying itself into the earth and resurrecting itself as a new tree.

The soil represents the life on earth. It is in the ocean of human relationship that the seed spreads roots through its experiences and accumulated knowledge and wisdom, and it shoots up to the light to communicate with all those who were fortunate enough to break through the limitations of human life.

Thus we are not immortals. Immortality is not a gift but a most precious possession gained by self-exertion and by increasing the fire and building up the diamond soul.

Every human soul is a fiery nucleus in which is found the path of possibility to reach to the stars. Nothing can stop the creativity of man when the fiery diamond soul is constructed in his higher mental plane.

It is this diamond that is immortal, and it is this diamond soul that has the power to build higher vehicles to contact higher states of consciousness and existences. Sometimes human forms, when their time of opportunity is over, disintegrate in the etheric, astral, or mental plane — according to the fire they have.

The Monad in the human form is not a nucleus of fire or an atom but a ray of life, a "tree." It is after *individualization* that a living form can develop the selfhood, the "fruit." The fruit has an opportunity to develop selfhood, an independent center of life upon the lifeline of the *Monad.*

This opportunity has a certain duration of a few thousand or a few million years, in which the individualized human soul must develop the consciousness of selfhood, a human soul.

It is this period of opportunity that can be used or misused. If the period of opportunity is used to increase the fire, in creating fiery thoughts, fiery words, fiery actions, then the formation of the human soul proceeds.

But if the human thoughts, words, and actions are not charged by pure fire, they become devices of destruction for the human soul in construction or in formulation.

When the time of opportunity is over and the formation of the human soul has not reached the degree in which new opportunities can be given to him, then the process of disintegration takes over and man begins to "lose his soul."

This is why Christ warned: *For how would a person be benefited, if he should gain the whole world and lose his own soul? Or what shall a person give in exchange for his soul?*[1]

M.M. says: *Soulless people are known to all. This is not a figure of speech, but a chemical reality.... The dissipation of Agni [the fire] occurs in everyday life when the spirit slumbers.*[2]

1. Matt. 16:26
2. Agni Yoga Society, *Fiery World,* Vol. I, para. 138.

The spirit here is the human soul in construction. When the human soul "slumbers," which means when he does not think, speak, or act through the currents of fire, the dissipation of the fire takes place, and the flame of the human soul is eventually extinguished.

M.M. suggests that one does not need to take extraordinary actions to build his soul — the fire within — but he needs to nourish his soul daily with lofty thoughts, express loving and harmless words charged with wisdom, and engage himself in constructive, creative labor.

The individual soul will eventually grow to the likeness of a tree and eventually will fuse with the Whole Self consciously.

14

The Progress of Our Soul

What have we done in the past for the progress of our soul? Some people have physical problems, emotional problems, and mental problems. And sometimes they seek the causes of these problems at the wrong address.

There is a very important cause of our troubles that we can explain in this way: There are some kinds of fruits in which the kernel grows but the shell does not grow. The shell prevents the growth of the core. The shell is the physical body, the emotional body, and the mental body. It is traditions, your knowledge, your philosophy, your psychology. It is your money, your dollars, your possessions, your car. These are the shell. The shell is so hard that it does not allow the core to radiate out or to bloom. And because the core is strong and eventually breaks the shell, it causes lots of trouble in the shell. It cracks it. And this cracking is your problems, your emotional problems, physical problems, and mental problems.

There is something in you that is trying to grow and you are preventing it. Of course, to hear these things is very easy because our ears do not have doors. The words enter from one and leave by the other.

This is really the situation. You can think for months and years about what your problem is, but in reality you are resisting the development of something within you.

And the second situation is just the opposite: Sometimes your outer shell grows so large that eventually you search for the core and you cannot find any. The outer shell emptied, finished, devoured it, and there is no core in that human being. It is finished. These are the people we can call coreless people.

Coreless people are so common. They look very beautiful. They dress so beautifully. Their philosophy is so beautiful. They worship and speak about God and Christ millions of times daily, and they carry the Bible on their heads. But what really do they do? If you search for any core, there is no core. There is no factuality, reality in them. You touch them and they are empty. And because the core cannot sustain itself forever (I want you to understand the symbolism of this) and the shell does not receive any nourishment anymore, it starts cracking. I have seen this kind of cracking.

For example, suddenly you see that a worshipful man who was going to church every day does something so shameful. What happened? One of the layers cracked. That man who was so philosophical starts writing trash and thinks that he can escape from the death that he is spreading. And that man who was so strong physically suddenly collapses. Why? You search and search and say that he has that sickness, this sickness. He has no sickness! There is no core to sustain the shell.

It is so serious, deplorable, sad, even good that you have sickness so that you learn that you are not going to put yourself in a shell at the expense of your essence. And your essence must find the freedom to grow within the shell that protects the core and to become its nourishment. Eventually all outer manifestations symbolically become the outer expressions of the beauty that the inner core is radiating out.

There is a core, an idea, and there is the language through which you are trying to express. If these two things are really harmonized, you become a human being. Not before. Your core is there to sustain the personality, and personality is there to translate the core. Any time you have any trouble — physical trouble, emotional trouble, mental trouble — you must think about these two symbols.

Ask yourself first, "Are my outer expressions and manifestations, being, and existence growing at the expense of the core?"

For example, a man sells his soul to make money, and he is involved so much that he has no time to think about his soul. He is getting rich, but when a time comes and the Guardians of the Gate examine him as he is leaving his body, they will find nobody. And if the "nobody" is found, he has "knowledge" but he is nobody. And this is the collapse of the human soul at the gate of the death.

Man must grow outside and inside, harmoniously, beautifully, so that he uses the outside to spread the blessings of the inner core.

And what is that inner core? That inner core is you, if you are there. It is you, the soul. The soul manifests and builds a physical body, and the soul builds the emotional body so that he acts in that body, feels with that instrument. Then he builds another mechanism that is called the mental body to think, to relate, to appropriate, to find, to discover, to answer. Then he tries to master these instruments and adapt them to a greater need of the Universe, to a greater communication with Cosmos. Eventually he masters these things — physical body, emotional body, mental body. He wins the power to enter the other realms consciously and eventually recreate himself, his body, his emotions, his mind to such a degree that they are immortal. The outer shell became immortal because the outer shell is transfigured, totally transfigured.

How can you develop the inner core? You can start developing the inner core and outer shell in harmonious ways only by checking yourself daily, observing yourself physically, emotionally, mentally, and then adapting yourself to those situations that are not antagonistic to the development of your core.

To do these observations here are a few questions for you. If you ask these questions and try to answer them, you will start bugging your core and yourself and find a way to develop your soul. They are very easy questions. They are not philosophical; they are common sense.

The first question is this: *Am I really conscious about my future?* It is so interesting. If you start a car and I ask you, "Where are you going?" and you say, "I don't know," that is crazy. Yet, that is the situation. Most of us do not know where we are going. And the pitiful thing is we think that we know. That is where the self-deception and hypocrisy start. You think you know where you are going.

One man who knew where he was going was a criminal. I went to the prison and he was going to be sitting in the chair. I said, "Where are you going? Do you know?" "Torkom," he said, "into eternal suffering." "How do you know? Did you know before? "No," he said. "That is why I am going there. God, you are so beautiful."

Even the religious man, the saved man, the worshipful man does not know where he is going. The condemned man did not say he was going to paradise. Let us see where he is going.

So the first question you are going to ask very sincerely is Where am I going? Where am I going with this activity, with these kinds of emotions and feelings and attitudes? Where am I going with these thoughts, this kind of thinking? Where am I going? Am I going beyond that?

The second question is *Am I maturing?* Are you maturing? When you are building a house, every day you go to see if it is being completed. If you plant a tree, every day you are going to see if the tree is growing. If you have a little child, every day you expect he is growing a little. Why are you not thinking about your soul, whether it is growing or not? Did you think about it?

Either my soul is growing or I am fooling around.

Am I repeating my mistakes, physical mistakes, emotional mistakes, mental mistakes, worrying mistakes? Am I really doing it again?

What is a mistake? Things that I do not like to do, I am doing again. Are you increasing your mistakes or decreasing? Well, if you are decreasing it is okay. If you are increasing you are becoming more shell and less core.

The next one: *Did I gain more control over my habits, negative emotions, harmful thoughts, and words?* Did I gain more control over my habits? Some people even do not know they are habits because they are machines and a machine does not know how it is functioning. Somebody else must look at the machine and say, "You are awkward." If you want to look into the machine, you are going to see how you are functioning. What are my habits? Sex habits, eating habits, drinking habits, cursing habits, depression habits, hating habits, and you name them, millions of them. Am I gaining control over them? Am I gaining control over my words? Is my yak, yaking, slandering, malicing so important or am I gaining more control over them?

What about my thoughts? Do I have more harmful thoughts or less? This is a problem. Some people think you kneel down and you say, " I wish you to do that for me." We want everybody to help us. What are you doing? Pay for it. The Universe does not give anything to you except if you pay for it. Your bank cannot even do that. The bank gives money, but then it asks 25% interest. What about the bank of the Universe? Think about it.

Do I see a meaning in life? Is there any meaning? Meaning means the "why" of why am I here.

For some people this is the hell in which they are living. For some people it is a school. For some people it is a stage to dump their problems. For some people it is to make money and die under the load. For some people it is a serious school, and they come here and they are anxious to learn their lessons every day. And life provides them. Your boyfriend, girlfriend, your pains and sufferings, experiences, and events are textbooks of lessons. If you read them carefully, you learn how to read. If you just go over the pages, as a student once did, you get nothing. The teacher asked the student if he had gone over his book. He said, "Yes." "But you don't know what is says." The boy said, "I put it on the floor and jumped over it." He jumped over it. And if you go over it, you have no development. You are cheating yourself as surely as if you were taking one hundred dollars from the hand of a little boy and putting it in your pocket. You feel so sorry, but that is what you are doing to yourself — stealing from this pocket and putting in that pocket.

Am I more giving? My gosh, more giving. Some people, if you one or two dollars from them, it is better that you cut their heart than take from them two dollars. I have seen such people. They do not even pay what they owe. Give. Life is created to teach you giving. Do not cheat yourself. Give what? Give your service, your beauty, your intelligence, your wisdom, your love, your compassion, your money, your property.

Why is giving so important? They will teach you why at the end of your life. They will make you stand there and then say, "Aha, are you giving up everything or not?" Learn it from love. Give so that you learn. They say, "Come and give again." "Yes, I don't want anything. I gave it up, my property, everything."

Somebody was dying from cancer. At the last minute he wanted Holy Communion from me. I said, "Okay, open your mouth." "Torkom," he said, "What about my property?" "You are crazy," I said. "All the property that you have is your body and you are leaving it." He said, "That is the best part. I want to take it with me."

It is humorous, but it is so sad. That is why I grew a little wiser after seeing these kinds of things in the hospital.

What are you giving? Are you helping all the movements in the world — whether it is your church, your government, any group, anything? I do not have any discrimination, but help them if they are working on the line of Beauty, Goodness, Righteousness, Joy, and Freedom. Help them. If you do not help them, your darkness will get you. So really help them.

Why to help? It is the greatest law in the Universe that if you receive and do not give, you die. That is the symbol of breathing. Life is breath; giving is life. Can you give more?

Take it and give it. Take it and give it. What happens? You see that your blood is energized. In taking and giving you have more life than if you give without taking or when you take and do not give.

I remember what Christ said about putting money in the little box of donations. Some man came and put one hundred dollars in the box and left. Everybody knew that the man was putting in a hundred dollars. A little old lady came and put in five cents. I really wondered how Christ knew that it was five cents or ten cents. Suddenly one day I found out. One day I received some change and dropped it in a box. One penny, ten pennies. It was from the sound exper. that ≠ body

that He knew what they had left. But the important part was that the man gave very little compared to what he took from life, while the old lady gave all that she had. She was in balance — taking and giving.

Here is a difficult question. *Did you ever experience that you are not the body?* If you have not had this experience, hurry. Was it real? I went to monasteries, here, there, read many, many books, really read them. I went to lectures, this or that. One day the teacher told me that I was going to speak about immortality. I said, "Of course." I went home. I brought all my books down, writing, reading, taking notes until early morning. I became insane. I said, "What are you saying? You don't know anything about it." I called the priest and said, "I can't talk." He said, "Why?" "I don't have any experience." "Just talk," he said, "people are waiting." I said, "No, I can't." Until I had an experience and succeeding experiences, I did not want to open my mouth about that. Until you have some real, factual knowledge and experience that you are not the body, you do not know that, and all that you are building the wind will come and take away.

Do I consider that life does not end with the earthly incarnation? Do I see this? Or is this it? No, this is not it. Why not? All the books and lectures say it is not. They say it. Do they test it? A tape recorder says many things, but a tape recorder never grows. I go to the lectures and sit and two hours later I still did not grow. You have millions in every city, here and there — tape recorders. There is nothing that they do not know. Everything is not okay because a tape recorder tells you nothing.

What we are talking here is actual, factual search for experience. It is not easy.

One day a lady was pregnant and I was making jokes. "Torkom," she said, "I wish that one day you have a child and you will know what it means." That is what we are talking about. That is where the power is, where the beauty is, where the influence is.

Do I have a planned study? Okay, you want to be an engineer. That is fantastic. You want to be a doctor. That is fantastic. You want to be a politician, a president. Fantastic. But did you think about your soul and how that soul must be the Supreme? And what studies are you doing to achieve that goal?

Planned study is not just going to the book shelves and saying this is magic, this is witchcraft, this is cultish, this is this, this is that. You cannot reach anywhere without systematized reading. "This year I am going to read these two, three books and really chew them." Systematized study is lacking in the United States. Immediately people find trash, they devote all their life to that trash. Immediately they find something beautiful, for two days maybe they study, but the third day they go and nothing happens. They do not have serious, continuous study, planned study. They invited me to a commune. They said, "Come and see our commune." I went to the commune. The girls and boys of those adults were so unhealthy. I said, "What is this? Do you have a plan of study here? It should be like a school. Two hours before, two hours after eating at night, planned study that you learn something. Do you have it?" "No."

Do you have a plan for meditation? "Meditation? What do you mean? Oh, sometimes I lie down and hallucinate, repeat mantrams, and that is my meditation." Wait until you reach the Gate. Planned meditation, sensible, rational, logical, reasonable, something that fits in this age of science, in this age of politics, life, difficulties, problems. Do you have something like that?

A woman wrote to me. She said that for five days she was crying. Believe me, yesterday I received that letter. I said, "Why are you crying?" She said, "Because my black cat died." I said, "That is wonderful. I really appreciate this. When you die, who is going to cry for you?"

Did you organize yourself to do really sensible meditation so that you meet the problems of life in greater maturity, in greater understanding? Well, that kind of meditation gives you that kind of power. Do you have it? You do meditation one day and ten days you forget; one month you did it, ten years before that. This is the problem. Without consistent study and meditation you cannot nourish and make your soul progress.

Everything in the Universe grows from the core; nothing grows from the shell. The shell is the waste of the core if you really, philosophically understand it. A man came here asking questions of me for three hours. I was forced in a way to answer him. "What can I do to make this business, that business...." And the summary was this, "How can I arrange my life in such a way that I can make more money?" After three hours I wrote something and gave it to him. I said, "Unless the values of your core increase, the shell you are building will vanish in front of your eyes." And he said, "That is not what I came here for." I said, "That is not what you want but it is what I want to give you." Planned meditation, study....

Do you really realize that whatever you are, whatever the situation is, whatever the condition is, it is the one that you can control? It is for your creativity. Do not let anybody else handle it. Do you have that understanding? Once you have that understanding you will collect all your energies to change and sublimate and make yourself beautiful. Every time we open our mouth, we blame somebody else, some events, some dates, some person, even we blame the birds that sing and awaken us. "That is why I failed my job." I know about such kinds of things.

Are you going to realize sincerely that whatever you are now — physically, emotionally, mentally, your home situation, your financial situation, your position in society, everything that you have — is what you wanted to create and you created it? Unless you understand that, you will be walking with blindfolded eyes. You are not understanding the big, real issue.

Another question to ask is *Am I grateful for all the help that I received from everywhere?* Are you grateful? A boy wrote to me from Agoura, California. He said, "Whatever I do I am unsuccessful." I answered, "There is no gratefulness in your heart." This happened two months ago. He wrote me another letter and said, "I am now exercising gratefulness, and really I am doing my best." Two days ago I received another letter. He found a new job and is making tremendous money. Look how he changed. The shell changed when the core changed.

Are you grateful? A lady came here to hear the lecture and she was not smiling. Somebody asked her outside, "What do you think about it?" She said, "I don't like him because...." I do not want to say the word she used. She was ungrateful.

You must increase your gratitude if people bug you more. If they create difficulties, outrages within you, they are your real friends.

Q&A

***Question:** I don't understand how when you are in a situation in your life that you created that situation.*

Answer: Because every kind of situation you have personally in your life is the result of how you thought, how you felt, how you acted, how you decided, how you discriminated, how you functioned.[1] This is very difficult to accept. That is why I said that it is very difficult to see. And we do not know it. We do not like to say "I failed" because the word is not good. "I didn't educate myself because of my mommy, my grandma, my stepmother, brother, this or that." You blame others. And because you blame five million addresses instead of yourself, you never come to yourself and realize that you are the cause. You missed the core, and then

1. See also *Karma and Reincarnation.*

when you miss the core, you cannot create new results. It is very deep. It is not easy.

You think that because you are not healthy it is the result of something outside of you. It is mostly you — because you did not know what to think, how to relate, or with whom to go, with whom not to go, what to drink, what not to drink. Why were you not excited? Why were you excited? Why were you irritable? Why were you not irritable? These kinds of things are accumulations, and accumulations have results.

If what I am saying does not convince you it is because until you have a breakthrough, you do not awaken. Suddenly you have a breakthrough that "I am reaping whatever I sowed." What says the good book? The good book says, "Whatever you sow, you will reap." Wise people know that.

Question: How do you experience immortality?

Answer: Meditation. Actually, really meaningful meditation is to pull yourself from the domination of the body, emotions, and mind and withdraw into higher spheres and suddenly see that you are sitting there. "What is that body? Is it me?" Then you will come back. We are not teaching these things yet because you are not ready for it. You are not.

Two years, three years we are here, and not one cabbage came here and said, "I want to progress. I really want to find immortality." They came and asked, "My girlfriend, do you know what I should do?" Okay. If that is the important thing in your life, you have it. What really is the important thing in your life? It is your soul. That is the Jewel within you. Christ told that story. It is so beautiful. People did not understand what He was talking about. Actually, if there is anybody in the world who is not understood, it is Christ.

There was a rich man. Who is the rich man? It is the outer shell. He had reputation, position, clothing, everything. That is the rich man. Suddenly he says, "There is some land and in that land is a jewel. My goodness," says the rich man, "I must go and sell everything I have to buy that land to get that jewel." What does it mean to sell? It means to give up. That is you. Find your jewel, yourself. And if you can, sell everything, which means to sacrifice and renounce everything to find that jewel.

This also was taught by a great Chinese Master. A boy came to the Chinese Master and said, "Can I learn in your monastery?" The Master said, "Yes, my son." He said, "Come here and enter the river." So the boy entered the river and it was four, five feet deep. The Teacher put his hand on the boy's head and pushed the boy under the water. "One, two, three, four, five, six." The boy is dying. "Eight, nine, ten." He came up. Then the Teacher asked, "Why did you come up? What were you really aspiring and striving for while under the water?" He said, "Air." "Well," the Teacher said, "if you in just that way search for the Teaching, it will be given to you."

But you did not come to that stage yet because you are fooling around with the fish.

Question: *You stressed the importance of giving, giving based on the five principles — Beauty,*

Goodness, Righteousness, Joy, and Freedom. What happens when you can't find a place, a job worth giving to?

Answer: Yes, I'll tell you something. I am not referring to you. I and another friend went to Paris. When we arrived the friend said, "I am going to disappear. Do anything you want." I said, "Fine. That is what I wanted. Give me space and freedom." So he went and I went. Where did I go? I went to the Notre Dame of Paris. I cried. The color, the shapes, something was transforming me. The next day I went to the ballet, the next day to the symphony, the next day something else, museums. I came home crying. And I was so tired that I fell asleep. He came and awakened me. "Torkom, I know you were fooling around. That is why you are tired." I said, "Shh, leave me alone."

Next morning when I awakened, I asked, "Where were you?" "You know," he says, "Paris is nothing else but a whore house. What do you think about it?" "No," I said, "Paris is a place of Notre Dame, music, symphony." "You are kidding," he said.

What is the difference between that man and me? Each searched for what he wanted to find. If you cannot find a place where you can put your heart and money except at your home, too bad. Beauty exists. Greatness exists. Nobility exists. But you are going to find them. And do not make excuses that you did not give that five dollars because it was not worth it. We can deceive ourselves like that also. I deceived myself. That is why I know.

So the Teaching is hard, really hard — the Teaching we are giving here. There is no flattery, no bribery. I really say things I want to say even if you crucify me.

In Zurich I was talking to somebody and he insulted my country, I said, “You son of a bitch, get out of here. Who are you to insult my country. And he was a psychiatrist. He walked off immediately. That is what you must do.

You find exactly what you want to find. That is the discrimination we are talking about.

Why did I not go to the whore places? I was dreaming about the Notre Dame. I must find it and see it because thousands of very sublimated artists and engineers worked to produce it. I wanted that thoughtform. But my friend went and sold himself. May God be with him.

Note: First printed in part in *Challenge for Discipleship*, Ch. 28.

15

The Golden Bridge

Man is conscious only on the fourth level of the mental plane. Below this level is the subconscious mind, which he has left behind. Beyond the fourth level are the third, second, and first levels of the mental plane — the higher mind into which man seldom penetrates.

It is possible to build a bridge between the fourth level and the higher mind and thus become aware of the life going on at these levels. On the fourth level of the mind there is a nucleus of light called the mental unit. On the highest level there is another nucleus called the Mental Permanent Atom. A bridge composed of mental substance must be built between these two poles.

This structure is called the Golden Bridge — a path of light extending between these two points. When a human being starts to build this Bridge, we say that he is traveling on the Path. In esoteric literature, this bridge-building process is likened to that of the spider that spins its web externally from the silk it produces internally, extending its thread from within to without. As man travels on the Path, which in Sanskrit is called the Antahkarana, he slowly enters into greater light.

On the fourth level of the mind we have four centers: the base of spine, the generative organs, the solar plexus, and the spleen. When man travels into the third level, he contacts a field of electricity that is the field of the Chalice, or Lotus. As his contact with the Chalice deepens, he slowly becomes Soul-infused.

The developing human soul, which is the "fallen Spark," builds a Path and extends himself toward the next station on the Path, which is the Mental Permanent Atom. Actually, the Path is nothing more than the extension of the developing and unfolding human soul. This is why one Great Master said, "I am the Path."

The Path is built by our victories over our weaknesses, by our realizations, actualizations, and spiritualizations. As you spiritualize yourself, as you actualize your inner glory and advance from darkness to light continuously, you will build the Path. The Path is not built by reading books or by acquiring knowledge. No activity, religion, or philosophy creates the Path. The Path is the steady transmutation, transformation, and transfiguration of the unfolding human soul. What you see when you look at a comet is the lighted trail that it leaves; the lighted trail of the comet is the comet itself. In the same way, man is his own illuminated Path.

When a flower begins to bud, it has no perfume. But as the bud begins to flower, the perfume hidden within the heart of the flower begins to release itself, becoming stronger and stronger as the flower opens. A human being, like the flower, becomes radioactive and fragrant with love, harmlessness, understanding, humility, power, persistence, endurance, and selflessness.

A man can be known by his fragrance. This is not a symbolic statement. The aroma emitted by a human being changes each step along the way. We do not smell good when we are in the animal kingdom or when we are in the human kingdom and we behave like animals. When a human being is criminal, when he is jealous and hateful, full of aggressive and destructive emotions and thoughts, he smells terrible. Human animals also cast dark, dirty, and ugly shadows.

But as man enters the Path, his service, his serenity, his beauty, and his fearlessness — in a word, his perfume — steadily increase until the time comes when he becomes a path for others. In a beautiful mantram we are told, "I am a way by which men may achieve."[1] The evidence that a man has actually built the Bridge is his steadily increasing love nature and his ability to think clearly. These two qualities always go together.

An average man or aspirant who is not yet on the Path allows his mind to think for itself, so to speak. He does not control his mind but allows it to run on automatic. A man on the Path uses his mind; he thinks through his mind rather than allowing his mind to think mechanically. A man on the Path learns to purify his mind from automatic actions and reactions. He does his own thinking. His mind becomes steadily, increasingly under his control as he travels the Path until it is eventually completely under his control.

Christ said, "By their fruits you will know them." What are these "fruits"? They are the expressions of our nature. If we speak about beauty but in the meantime behave in ugly

1. Mantram of the Disciple. See also *Discipleship in the New Age*, Vol. 2, p. 175, by Alice A. Bailey.

ways, then we are not on the Path and we do not produce good fruit. A sign of having built the Path is that we go through a process of self-actualization, self-expression, and self-becomingness. Our inner glory becomes individualized and materialized, and it manifests itself.

The Path is slowly built by all that we do, think, and feel. When we are in the process of building a house, nothing spectacular seems to happen for the first few months. Someone may even remark that we do not seem to be making much progress. But all along materials are being ordered and prepared. Suddenly, in what seems like a very short time, the house goes up. Similarly, every good word, every kind thought, and every sacrificial action accumulates to build the Golden Bridge. Dedication, simplicity, and humility add credit; these are the stones out of which a man builds his temple.

This is why good deeds are so highly regarded in holy scriptures. Each good deed is a drop of beauty emanating from the person's core like the sweet-smelling sap of a tree. Perhaps you have seen a person in distress, sitting and thinking in gloom. If you went over to him, touched him and said, "Peace be with you! Everything will be better tomorrow. Come on, my friend, take courage," you may think that this was a small thing; but it was a great and beautiful act.

If you even tried to help a little dying bird, you have recorded a wonderful deed in the Book of God because no act in life is ever without its effects. Perhaps in ten thousand years that bird will be in a position to help you in a moment of need. The universal computer of karma keeps such accurate calculations that even the smallest credits and debits are faithfully recorded.

We must never forget that all of Nature and space is an immensely intricate and accurate recording mechanism. Nothing is ever lost. We actually are living within the sight of a Great Presence.

At first man lives as though no one sees him. When he begins to travel the Path, he begins to sense that he is being watched. And when he approaches the end of his Path he says, "Everyone sees me." At this point in his development he plays his cards openly.

In order to travel the Path, the unfolding human soul must build the Path within his own mechanism. He builds the Golden Bridge on the mental plane using his own mental substance.

The mental body is a sphere of radioactive substance around the head and shoulders. This substance consists of seven increasingly-refined grades of material. The seventh level is very coarse, the sixth a little more refined, and so on. To make this easier to understand, suppose that I have dust of seven different colors in my hand. If I throw it into the air, the dust collectively forms a loose sphere and all the colors are intermingled. All of these particles of dust are mingled together, but because of their particular color, or frequency, each similarly colored particle is in electrical communication with every other particle of its own kind. Those grains of dust that are blue are on one plane; those that are yellow are on another plane; and those that are orange are on still another plane.

The three higher levels of the mental plane contain a center of energy that is referred to in esoteric literature as the *causal body*. It is also called the Lotus, or the main chakra. In the highest level of the mental plane is found, as was previously stated, a nucleus of light called the Mental Permanent Atom, and in the fourth level there is another seed of light called the mental unit. When these two points of light are related together and a communication line is established between them, man becomes a Path. We can then say that he has built his Golden Bridge from darkness to light, from the unreal to the real, from death to immortality, from chaos to beauty.

Immortality, the real light, and beauty are found on the higher mental plane in the Lotus or Chalice. This Chalice is the body of the Great Presence within us. As we travel the Path and enter into the spheres of the third, second, and first levels, our nature becomes transformed. We become a transfigured, Soul-infused personality. Our physical, emotional, and mental natures fuse with our Inner Presence and we sense that our body, emotions, and mind are under a different guidance.

As we come under the guidance of our Soul, a most important change takes place. The polarization of the atoms and cells of our bodies changes from being involutionary to being evolutionary. Instead of going toward materialization, condensation, and separation, the magnetism of the bodies changes and becomes polarized toward spiritualization and sublimation.

As this great change occurs in our physical, emotional, and mental bodies, our consciousness slowly awakens. When the Path is built from the fourth level of the mental plane to the third level, man realizes for the first time that there is another world beyond what he previously knew. At night when he sleeps he begins to penetrate to certain levels where classes are being held to study higher wisdom, and he can attend with the groups of people there. At this point man realizes that the life he was once living was only one percent real and that ninety-nine percent of his life was illusion. He now knows that there is something much greater waiting beyond his daily life.

On the fourth level of the mental plane there is much conflict. A man who lives on the fourth level is like a fish who can occasionally leap out of the ocean for a quick glance at the sky before sinking back into the depths. Man on this level is a shadow, a flickering light. He vacillates between love and hate, between jealousy and dedication, between selfishness and generosity. He is very unstable and does not know in which direction Home is.

On the fourth level of the mental plane, man is uncertain and unsteady. He is afraid that if he goes toward light, toward greater selflessness and sacrifice, he will lose everything in his life. For example, he is afraid he will lose his girlfriend because he does not realize that if he loses her on the lower level he will win her again at a higher level. And in the higher levels he will recognize her not only as a physically attractive body but also as a beautiful mind and spirit.

The evolution of man's spirit is very natural. Just as we once attended kindergarten and were taught at that level and then gradually proceeded onward to high school and to other schools of higher learning, we also learn and progress on the spiritual path. Progress in the subjective life is as inevitable and as real as any progress made in earthly education. In spiritual education we meet those who lead us toward greater beauty and self-actualization. And just as we are obliged by our local laws to attend school and take certain courses until we reach a certain age, so does the great Inner Government that oversees the spiritual education of humanity determine our spiritual age and provide the appropriate training.

An average man who has not yet received a spiritual education thinks that life is his own to do with as he pleases — to waste or even to destroy if he so chooses. But as man progresses on his Path, he begins to realize that his life should be shared with others. He begins to realize that he does not belong to himself; he develops a sense of responsibility and cooperation. When he progresses still further, he realizes that his life does not belong to him at all but that it belongs to a Great Power — and he decides to obey the Will of that Great Power. He no longer belongs to himself because he realizes that he is a cell in the vast body of the Cosmos.

When man knows that he is a minute part of an immense "machine," he also knows that he has a vital part to play because he understands that the smallest malfunction in an intricate engine can ruin it. When a man realizes that he functions as a small bolt or screw in a great mechanism, he strives to keep himself in good working order. He wants to live in harmony with the rhythm of the greater mechanism. Just as our cells form our body, so it is that we form part of the Body of the great Cosmos. And it is necessary for every part of that Body to be healthy if the Body as a whole is going to be healthy.

As man progresses on the Path, tremendous changes are in store for him. When he succeeds in building the Bridge between his mental unit and his Mental Permanent Atom, he will have a unified field. There is no more death. There is no longer "sleep" and "waking." He is conscious on two levels simultaneously. Initially he has this experience once or twice in his lifetime; then it becomes several experiences a year. Eventually a time comes when he is always awake. At this stage he can communicate with his own group, with his Master, or even think along two lines at the same time. He can talk to an audience and simultaneously answer his Master's questions. This is a great achievement, and all great disciples have accomplished it.

These kinds of spiritual achievements never are possible through the use of marijuana, LSD, hashish, or any other drug.[2] No mechanical or artificial means can lead human beings to reality on higher levels. Man grows from within — never from without. As his consciousness grows and expands, a man's mechanism builds upon it. But his mechanism cannot build or transform his consciousness. And if the inner pressure does not change, eventually the outer shell cracks.

When man builds the Golden Bridge, another great expansion occurs. We are told that during the Third Initiation, the Bridge extends from the Mental Permanent Atom to the Intuitional Permanent Atom and to the Atmic Permanent Atom. These three form the Spiritual Triad. When a

2. See *Fiery Carriage and Drugs.*

man enters into the Intuitional Plane, he becomes aware of the Plan and Purpose of the Planetary Logos.

Higher contacts develop in the same way that our human relationships do. At first the contacts are brief. But as time goes on, meetings are lengthened and contacts are amplified. For example, your Master first acknowledges you in a brief greeting. Then later He takes you into His group and, still later, into His classes.

Greater realities are in store for us if we strive to meet the requirements. The first requirement is that each day we should remember to live a life of real compassion. This is the practical side of the building process because the first energy that urges us to expand and build the Bridge is the energy of compassion. To smile, to bless, to love, to help and sacrifice, and to keep this voltage of high energy within us all of the time is the daily path on which we must walk. If a human being can live in such compassion for as short a time as thirty days, his Path will be built.

This kind of discipline creates a steady focus in your consciousness. Instead of being a flickering light, there is a steady light that controls your reactions in life. First, man learns to control his physical expressions. The spoiled monkey — the human mouth — is particularly difficult to control. Then comes the ability to control the emotional reactions and eventually the mental reactions. He then can steadily pour forth all that he has and is. To reach this level takes time, and we must not become discouraged on the path of our striving.

People are afraid of failure and are discouraged by it. They do not realize that failure is the greatest teacher —

even greater than a Master. When a person fails, his eyes are opened and he can learn. Failure can teach us when nothing else can. This does not mean that we should try to fail but that when we do fail, we should learn from our failure. We must never be discouraged. If our eyes are focused on the goal, no matter how many times we fail we will reach our goal sooner or later.

The question is: Do we have a vision of beauty upon which we can shape our lives? If we have a vision of beauty to follow, we will always be sane. The degree to which a vision of beauty is alive in our consciousness is the degree of magnetism that vision will have to draw us onward and transform us into our vision. Sometimes we have very small magnets leading us on: a romantic relationship, money, or knowledge. These are neither bad nor are they Ultimate Magnets — the supreme beauties that cause us to progress on the path of spiritual evolution.

The Path for man unfolds through striving and by conquering those obstacles that hinder his progress. According to the Ageless Wisdom, the greatest battlefield for man is the emotional plane. His most difficult battle is to overcome his own emotional reactions and turmoil. Because we are able to think, we sometimes naively believe that we are already mental beings and that we do not need to conquer our emotions. Then suddenly we are caught up in a whirlpool of emotional reactions and our blissful ignorance is rudely interrupted.

Emotions and mind are two completely different elements in our nature. We must experience what mind is and what emotion is, and we must learn how to distinguish between them. We feel love and hate at the same time and do not know why. But if we think about it and start to search for the cause and effect, then we are mentally active. This is the process of true knowing.

Automatic actions and reactions are emotional, but to understand this we need experience — and we must try to learn these lessons of experience without paying too heavily, without losing our lives. For example, a fellow who learns the difference between emotions and thinking by having sex with a girl who has syphilis will find that this lesson cost him dearly. He was carried away by his emotions and contracted a lasting disease — and afterward learned to think.

We tend to carry on many vices in the same way without thinking about their effects. We smoke, drink alcohol, and use drugs without ever analyzing what it is we are doing. This kind of behavior is entirely emotional because we act irrationally and are controlled by posthypnotic suggestions in these instances. We do not think when we do these kinds of things; we are not searching for the causes and effects, but are only acting spontaneously and reacting emotionally.

There are techniques to overcome emotional reactions that change the current of energy and raise its level. For example, if a thought of doing wrong enters into a holy man's mind, he immediately turns his mind to Christ, to Lord Buddha, or to any Great One and makes his body perform strenuous physical activity. This displaces the emotional energy and sends it to higher levels.

The best tool we have for transformation of consciousness from lower to higher levels is meditation. Meditation is the hammer that builds the royal road of continuity of consciousness. But meditation must be real, scientific, and esoterically tested meditation. Those who sincerely want to change their nature, to become saner, clearer, and healthier, should carefully read *The Science of Meditation*.[3]

The goal of meditation is to make you mentally more radioactive, creative, and beautiful. It is the technique of mastering the whole mechanism of your mind and learning how to operate this complicated mechanism. It is not self-hypnosis or repeating a mantram until you nicely fall asleep.

Real meditation is a process of scientific thinking. It is through right thinking that we are able to expand our consciousness and build the Bridge with our compassion. It is a way to live a life charged with Beauty, Goodness, Righteousness, Joy, Freedom, Striving, and Sacrificial Service.

The greatest success a man can accomplish is the completion of the Golden Bridge. It is only across this Bridge that man can walk into supermundane realms.

3. By Torkom Saraydarian.

16

The Rainbow

We love rainbows. They give joy to us and bring peace into our hearts. We love beautiful things in Nature because pleasant memories are connected with them.

All that is in Nature is within us. Certain things make us feel pain and suffering because of painful memories attached to them. We love rainbows because everyone, unconsciously or consciously, tries to complete the rainbow within.

A rainbow, we are told, is a symbol of peace between the Most High and the world. Man, too, needs such peace between his divine and human nature.

A rainbow is not only a symbol of peace but is also a symbol of continuity of consciousness within the seven planes of existence in man and in Nature. The seven colors of the rainbow are the seven planes of the Cosmic Physical Plane.

The rainbow in each human being is of different magnitudes. Some of them are like the tiny rainbows of a sprinkle, of a fountain, or of a waterfall. There are also rainbows that embrace a few hills, a few mountains. Some of them reach high up to the sky, with distinct and deep colors. All human striving has one principle goal: to build a larger and larger rainbow.

Clairvoyants tell us that, viewed subjectively, every human being radiates spheres of colors. Some of these spheres are cloudy and mixed, with pale colors. Some of the spheres are clear, geometrical, concentric, and are very bright and luminescent. These are the glorious spheres of those who have made great spiritual achievements and have a past life of heroic service for humanity. Those who have murky or cloudy spheres are those whose lives are full of contradictions, crimes, or inertia. One day all human beings will be diagnosed through the conditions of their sphere of colors.

Man in essence is like a sun that radiates rays of light of seven colors. The rainbow around him is caused by the refraction and reflection of these rays of the Inner Sun in his etheric, astral, and mental "drops" or "atoms." The Inner Sun, radiating through the primordial substance around it, creates seven layers of colors, that slowly darken and disappear as the "sun" starts its process of incarnation and draws to itself the etheric and physical materials.

Similarly, every Spark is a rainbow, a sphere of seven colors, having a bright light at the center that is a spark of God "more radiant than the sun."

These seven spheres of color, which are observed by the human eye, are as follows:

1. Red
2. Orange
3. Yellow
4. Green
5. Blue
6. Indigo
7. Violet

Every plane or vehicle of man has a color. Red is the color of the divine vehicle. Orange is monadic, yellow is atmic, green is buddhic, blue is mental, indigo is astral, and violet is etheric.

The hues of the colors change when a person takes initiation. There are seven initiations, which, like seven octaves of the musical scale, have forty-nine notes or levels. From the first to the second initiations, a threshold of colors slowly appears in the aura. The colors are not clear and bright but are fuzzy and mixed. In the Third Initiation, which is the first real initiation, clear color starts to appear, not only in the seven vehicles but also within each of the seven levels of each plane or vehicle.

In the Fourth and Fifth Initiations, the forty-nine colors synchronize. All levels of each of the seven vehicles synchronize with each other in harmonious hues. At the Ninth Initiation, man appears as a completed sphere of rainbow color. At this initiation, the rainbow has a nine-mile radius.

Thus, we have seven colors on each plane that synchronize with each color of each plane, and the symphony of the forty-nine colors becomes complete.

The ancients used to say that planets and stars were, once upon a time, human beings. As they took Cosmic Initiations, their sphere of colors extended miles and miles and they gradually attracted matter and atomic lives to themselves from space and formed spheric globes that served as schools to help the atomic lives advance in their education and build up their own rainbow.

In Nature we have permanent atoms that record all that is going on in all planes. They record all our thoughts, words, and actions like a super-sensitive photographic film. These permanent atoms are responsible for the quality of our health, well-being, creativity, and intelligence. Each time we take incarnation, our Inner Sun radiates through these atoms and creates on the physical plane an "image" that corresponds to what has been "photographed" in the permanent atoms. Man in his lower three worlds is exactly the projected image that is found collectively in the permanent atoms.

Permanent atoms register the history of man throughout eons by the changes occurring in the colors of the aura.

Joy, gratitude, honesty, and solemnity, for example, introduce very bright and deep colors in the aura, which scintillate with the heartbeat.

During such a rainbow manifestation, any fear, selfish action, hatred, greed, jealousy, or ill will takes away the beauty of the aura instantaneously and leaves it dull, muddy, or gray in color. The size of the aura shrinks and resembles aged skin.

Sometimes during such depression, germs attack and sickness develops. Psychic energy withdraws on such an occasion and the Temple remains open to dark attacks.

The permanent atoms register all these changes in their microcomputers. The Karmic Lords have direct access into these recordings.

To rebuild the beauty of the aura, we need to

1. make efforts to undo the wrongs committed
2. repent
3. meditate
4. save energy

5. pray
6. make a decision and resolution not to repeat the wrong actions anymore

Thus the aura begins to build again, but the previous depression is already recorded on the diskette.

Changes in the aura affect

1. plants
2. people's responses
3. events
4. electrical devices
5. the atmosphere of the room
6. reception of energy or prana
7. assimilation of prana

Changes are noticed in the throat, heart, and sacral centers and also in the eyes, voice, and in secretions of the glands.

The purity and clarity of each color of each body depends upon the contents of the permanent atoms. If the permanent atoms are pure and are not stained or polluted, the rays translate pure color and the bodies are formed with pure vibrations. But if the permanent atoms are not pure, the colors of each body do not manifest beauty and harmony.

Stains and pollution are accumulated in our permanent atoms or "diskettes" when we

- act wrong
- speak wrong
- feel wrong

- think wrong
- will wrong

or when we are forced by others to commit criminal acts, or when we are obsessed by entities that pollute and distort our communication network.

Many clairvoyants see slightly different colors in our vehicles — not because the individual colors change, but because the individual colors of layers of bodies fuse with the main color and change the coloring of the vehicle or plane of that vehicle if that vehicle is not yet mature and in tune within itself.

For example, let us take the original color of the mental body, which is blue. This blue color is a background of color on which we find seven premature colors that are component parts of the mental body. These seven colors — red, orange, yellow, green, blue, indigo, and violet — are the seven colors of the blue mental body.

Each vehicle has an original *drive* if it is pure, and there are seven associated *urges*. These drives can be labeled with the names of virtues, or let us say that each drive manifests through its vehicle as

1. perseverance
2. solemnity
3. enthusiasm
4. pure reason
5. creativity
6. pure sensitivity or feeling
7. action

When a vehicle is polluted or short-circuited, the corresponding virtue turns into a vice — and virtue fades away.

Each of these seven virtues is associated with seven comparative virtues. For example, the first virtue, which is perseverance, has seven hues, which are

1. daring
2. courage
3. stability
4. patience
5. determination
6. firmness
7. will power

The same is true for all the virtues.

Purity and harmony of the colors manifest as health, virtue, strength, creativity, and psychic development.

Impurity and inharmonious conditions of the colors create ill-health, vice, weakness, laziness or inertia, animalistic tendencies, and lower or dark psychism.

The health of each body is conditioned by the degree of the harmony found between the colors of that body. The health of all the vehicles is the result of harmony between the colors of all the bodies and the hues of the bodies.

Colors are nothing but qualities, virtues, or powers of each plane and subplane. The mixture of these colors makes the plane or the vehicle appear a different color. For example, if red and yellow combine, we have a predominant color of orange, and an inexperienced clairvoyant will have great confusion. If red and blue combine, we have purple. If yellow and blue combine, we have green. Violet stands above, as it is an etheric color and changes only through pranic mixtures. Thus we have red, yellow, and blue as primary colors.

The colors in your aura change continuously for the following reasons:

1. *Your thoughts.* The color of your thoughts depends upon what level of the mental body you think and with what interest you think. For example, you can think for physical interests, emotional interests, or spiritual interests.

2. *The purity of your vehicles or their contamination.* Purity lets the original color shine through. Contamination pollutes the color with the elements of the contamination.

3. *Positive and negative conditions or aspirations.* Remember that emotions are related to many interests. Also, negative emotions bring pollution while positive emotions help the original colors shine out.

4. *Your words or speech.* Remember that your speech can channel various kinds of virtues or vices, purity or pollution from many planes, and your speech can be true or false. False speech is like a stone that shatters a colorful window. A curse is like mud that is spread on a colorful canvas, or like water poured upon a bonfire.

5. *Actions.* Actions are expressions of your intent, purpose, and plan that can change the color of your aura. Sometimes your actions are controlled by other people's thoughts, emotions, and passions.

All of these have an effect on your rainbow. Thus, combinations of colors within your aura produce different shades of color in your aura, sometimes to such a degree that the whole original color of a vehicle or a plane totally becomes superimposed by a strange combination of colors.

When the seven radiations of the Inner Sun penetrate into the sphere of man, they create red, orange, yellow, green, blue, indigo, and violet layers of color. Actually, your divine body is red. Just around your Self there is a red halo. After that red, you have an orange halo, which is the Monadic Plane. Then there is the Atmic Plane, which is yellow, and the Buddhic Plane, which is green. The mental plane is blue, the astral plane is indigo, and the etheric plane is violet. This is not the case for all of us, however, because for most of us our bodies are still in formation and are mixed with many different kinds of emotions, fears, feelings, with revenge, jealousy, hatred, greed, glamour, and illusion — which also have color. For example, if the mind is thinking wrong, blue mixes with the colors of the negative thoughtforms and different color formations result in your aura. When your feeling and thoughts are mixed together and are radiating that mixture of colors that must be expressed through your emotional body, then the emotional body, which is indigo, radiates some kind of blue/yellow/orange color. This is why when you bring five clairvoyants together to look at a person, they each will see different colors in him. The reason for this is that they are seeing the different mixtures of colors in the aura through their own aura.

What happens when a person's aura develops? The sphere of the rainbow or the flower slowly expands. Expansion takes place first in the physical-etheric aura. Then the astral, mental, intuitional, atmic, monadic, and divine auras begin to expand, creating a wonderful synchronization of colors.

When all these primitive colors and their hues are fully developed, you will appear as an sphere of scintillating color and flashes of light. Your evolution starts from the lowest body, which is the etheric body. This body is violet with finer shades and hues. When your fourth etheric level begins to shine its color, the first level of the astral color begins to emerge.[1] Thus level after level, the colors emerge and their shades come into being until the divine body is formed. At that stage, you have seven main colors, or you have forty-nine shades.

In every second from the Central Core, seven colored energies flow into the aura and make the whole sphere of the aura palpitate like a heart. Each color and shade is like a note of the octave. Man, at first, sounds like waves or a waterfall. But then he slowly turns into noise, or chaos. As he advances in evolution, slowly all of his notes are tuned and when the tuning is complete, he becomes a rare symphony.

It seems impossible to describe how the similar notes of seven instruments — vehicles — synchronize and resonate with each other in different tempos, but in the same rhythm, to compose the symphony of the Rainbow.

Every man evolving toward perfection turns into a rare flower, a rare beauty with forty-nine colors or strings that resonate with the winds — the impressions — coming from the stars and constellations, bringing man and the Supermundane Spheres closer to each other.

1. See *The Science of Becoming Oneself,* p. 135.

The evolution of the aura is perceived in its colors and movements. First the colors flow clockwise, horizontally around the body. Then they turn and flow counterclockwise around the body. They then flow vertically from back to front. Next, the bands of colors expand, allowing more shades of color to enter between the main colors or planes. Slowly the aura changes into a series of vertical circles, with the center at the heart. It seems to turn clockwise as well as counterclockwise. The main colors turn counterclockwise as the hues or shades turn clockwise. All of this is over-powered by the seven ray emanations from the heart, which seem to provide the sparkling of the movement with rhythm.

As one passes from initiation to initiation, the aura expands and sometimes becomes so large that, like a rainbow, it penetrates into the sky, and as an umbrella of energy, it involves within its radius multitudes of people.

Thus, an Initiate brings blessings for many miles with His aura, providing an opportunity for people to find their path and direct their face toward Home.

Some people do not have a focused mind, a focused emotional body, or an integrated physical-etheric body. Such a condition makes their aura fluctuate continuously. People sense such auras and do not like to associate with them. Fluctuating auras create repulsion, and such people continuously lose their friends and their jobs.

Fluctuations of the aura have many causes. One of them is prostitution, where people make love with various people. They draw into their aura patches of the aura of the other person. As the forcing aura enters into their spheres of colors, it creates disturbances in them and the homogeneity of the aura suffers. This also causes a loss of magnetism.

Auric infection is a fact. Through mixed intercourse, a person draws into his aura the pollution of the other person and often is contaminated by various psychic disorders found in the other person's aura.[2]

Our aura is contaminated also when we associate ourselves with those who follow an unrighteous way of living. To help such people to continue their exploitation and to fulfill their greed is equal to a crime because through such associations the aura of all assistants becomes polluted.

Purity of the rainbow can be achieved by following the path of Beauty, Goodness, Righteousness, Joy, Freedom, Service, and in Striving toward perfection.

Your health, your strength, your creativity depend on the purity of the colors. If you take any one of these seven bodies and it is stained with something ugly and dirty, that body will not be healthy. If it is pure, that body will be healthy. When the body is healthy, it has a pure sound, a pure note. Each color is a sound. You radiate seven colors and seven sounds, plus their subtones and subhues. In the astral plane, entities will see your color. In the mental plane, they will hear your sound.[3]

As the color formation grows clearer and clearer, stronger and deeper, your tonality also increases, and these bodies build and unfold proportionately. This is why the Great Ones say, "We hear you." You can be loud or soft; you can

2. See *Sex, Family, and the Woman in Society.*
3. For further information, see *Aura, Shield of Protection and Glory* and *The Creative Sound.*

be a noise or a symphony. There will be distortion in your health, in your character, in your creativity, in your relationships, and in your sensitivity if the seven strings of your heart are not pure yet. We call this formation the process of alignment, integration, "symphonization." Eventually all of your forty-nine notes — the seven instruments playing seven notes each — create a symphony.

A symphony is the manifestation of divinity through all of your expressions. That is why we say that you must be physically, emotionally, and mentally healthy. If you are not healthy, your symphony cannot be built and come into manifestation. This is your ultimate goal in this incarnation. If you do not try to build the rainbow in this life, you are a failure in this life. You will return again and again to the worlds of suffering and pain until you complete this rainbow.

What happens if you do something wrong with one of your bodies? If you are doing wrong with your physical body (which is the expression of the etheric body), the color of the etheric body "evokes" each corresponding hue in the other bodies and induces disturbances in them. Any disturbance or sickness on any plane is shared by the whole aura. That is why you are a visible map for the eyes of the Great Ones Who watch you. There are seven sevens, or seven sublevels on each level of seven levels. Whatever is reflected in the lowest, or physical, level is reflected in the astral plane, the mental plane, the Intuitional Plane, the Atmic Plane, the Monadic Plane, and the Divine Plane. The distortion is carried into all seven planes. If you get syphilis on the physical plane, you have syphilis on all planes. You may cure syphilis on the physical plane, but you may still have syphilis on all the other planes that will slowly finish and exhaust itself on the physical plane. Exhaustion always occurs on the physical plane. You cannot cure it emotionally. The emotion must come to the physical plane and exhaust itself there. That is why the Great Ones say that karma is always a mess on the physical plane. Actually, we incarnate to exhaust our karmic liabilities on the physical plane.

Let us say that you said something wrong on the physical plane. You will immediately start showing the signs of distortion and confusion on the same corresponding level of all the other planes. Let us say that you have truth on one plane and that the truth is red. Then you create a lie on the emotional plane, which is, let us say, yellow. Yellow and red will mix together and create mixed colors in all the bodies. Now you are in a condition of chaos.

Whatever you do, whatever you speak, whatever you feel, whatever you think, you create impressions in the permanent atoms. These are your karmic liabilities, the wrong things you did that do not harmonize themselves with the color and the sound, with the symphony and harmony. Now you are going to take incarnation. The white light of the Inner Sun hits the permanent atoms and creates different colors in the bodies. It passes through a cloudy and messy condition that exists in the permanent atoms.

Let us say that your permanent atom in the astral plane is indigo, but because of the way you talk and because of your actions, it turns yellow. These permanent atoms are like genes which record everything that you speak, think, and feel. According to the quality of your thinking, doing, speaking, and acting, the color formation changes. Incorrect changes in the colors of the bodies are called perversion. When you incorrectly change the color of a body, you become perverted.

A virtue is a pure translation of the rays of the Self. For example, when these rays come from the Monadic Plane, they produce solemnity. If you are not solemn, it means that in a certain layer of each body there is something defective. As above, so below. If you do not have enthusiasm, it means that core electricity is not hitting the third plane and something is wrong with this body in the seven corresponding layers of the seven bodies. Something is breaking the energy flow and you are experiencing inertia or apathy because you blocked the rays and they are unable to vitalize your bodies. When there is no revitalization in the body, the seven centers and the seven senses in that body do not receive energy and they die, or they close like a bud. When your centers or senses in any plane are closed, you are dead in that plane.

Some people only live physically. In the Third Initiation, people are more alive. Before the year 2000 people must take the Third Initiation, undergoing a total purification of the mind, emotions, and body.

Color therapy will one day be a great science. The principal fact of color therapy is that whenever we observe a color, our aura changes into that color. But your concentration on the color provided differs according to the "eye" that you use to focus on the color.

For example, if there is a distortion of color in your etheric body and you are concentrating on a green color with your mental body, the "healing" of your etheric body will not take place. Instead, further complications will occur in your mind, creating further agitations in your etheric body.

It is easy to play with colors but one must know that each color is a chemical substance that must not be used in ignorance of its effect.

Each color must be "injected" in the right place, at the right dosage, to the right level, on the right plane. And this requires a highly-developed clairvoyant who will teach us what to do with color.

I remember an incident that occurred when a small group of people were playing music together. A boy with a saxophone entered and began playing the instrument as loudly as possible until all the other musicians eventually had to stop playing, wondering what was happening. Sometimes colors that are introduced can have the same effect on the bodies. This is why people must choose colors according to their evolution and need, and then change the colors of their environment when the focus of their consciousness begins to function on higher planes. It is the focus of consciousness that determines the strongest effect of the colors on the bodies.

Humanity as a whole must appear, when viewed from higher spheres, as a flower. But how will this flower be formed? Each individual human being must be a flower. Then each nation must be a flower having a human flower as a petal in its flower. All humanity will then be a flower, each nation serving as a petal in that glorious flower. Can you visualize the magnificent beauty of the flower of humanity, each petal formed by a flower of a nation and each nation as a flower formed by millions of people who have achieved at least the

Third Initiation? Can you visualize what an array of color, what a symphony we will project to space?

The physical body of humanity will start forming with millions of groups of the same color. The emotional body will form with the same frequencies of those groups that have the same color, and they will all synchronize in such a way that they will form one hue in seven different shades.

Each individual group will develop through simultaneous and unanimous meditation, study, and living the Teaching. Thus, eventually they will subjectively become one flower.

Do you see how much labor we have? That is why the Great Sage, speaking of labor, says, "Go and watch the starry skies and you will know how many millions of years you have to labor to reach there." You must remember that when the lower bodies act negatively or destructively, they send ugly messages to the higher bodies and create reactions from the Central Core. This reaction is a form of rejection of whatever it is that you are thinking, speaking, and doing.

Any sickness is an action of rejection of your pure Self. The Self rejects and pushes down to your physical body for manifestation all the dross that you send to the Self. This is called, in esoteric vernacular, reaction. Every negative condition in your physical, emotional, and mental bodies is a reaction coming from the Central Core and manifesting in one of your bodies. If the reaction hits your mental body, you will be insane. If it hits your astral body, you will be confused, irritated, and unstable. If it hits your physical body, you will have many kinds of sickness.

The reverse is also true. When the physical, emotional, and mental man is thinking, speaking, and acting in harmony with the keynotes of the planes, and when this reaches to the Central Core, there is a response that projects healing, uplifting, and purifying energies — or bliss — which a person feels when he is engaged in acts of Beauty, Goodness, Righteousness, Joy, and Freedom.

Every time a new Ray manifests, It creates either a powerful reaction or response from the threefold bodies of humanity, or from certain individuals or groups. Reaction creates storms in the mental, astral, and physical planes of humanity. This is exactly the case now. We are told that recently the Seventh Ray began to manifest due to the Law of Cycles and humanity is not ready to respond to it. It is the reaction of humanity to this Ray that is responsible for the widespread insanity, emotional imbalance, confusion, hatred, murder, and epidemics of disease that are prevalent in humanity today. A response from humanity would bring in the age that Utopians have dreamed about for many centuries.

This reaction by humanity is conscious and unconscious. It is the result of all of those thoughtforms that are criminal, separative, and destructive; the result of all emotions charged with hatred, fear, anger, jealousy, and revenge; the result of all those actions charged with the spirit of totalitarianism, greed, and exploitation. These elements are responsible for our reaction.

When the energy of the Seventh Ray hits all such polluted spheres, all the "bugs" of our nature are nourished and they multiply, creating the chaos that we now see existing all over the world. Humanity still survives because of a few "righteous" men who still exist on this planet. Remember the story of Lot!

But when your rainbow color formations become purer, deeper, and more perfectly synchronized in their motion and rhythm, then each vehicle becomes a transmitter for one of the Seven Rays.[4] Your whole rainbow becomes a harp on which these seven energies can play their Cosmic music, which means practically that you now have developed Cosmic consciousness.

How can we help humanity? The answer is to build the Rainbow Bridge and bring in divine bliss, joy, and peace to earth. Do whatever you can to restore Nature. Think in Light and Love. Live in Truth and Service. Know that humanity is like a man who must live a happy, healthy, prosperous life, and try to live for the happiness, health, and prosperity of humanity.

4. See *The Seven Rays Interpreted* video by Torkom Saraydarian.

17

The Causal Body

In ancient times the causal body was called "the temple not made by hands." It has also been called the ark, Noah's Ark, the Temple of Solomon, the twelve-petaled Lotus, and the Chalice. It has as many as twenty names, each with a slightly different meaning.[1]

The causal body is found in the mental plane. According to the Ageless Wisdom, the mental plane is divided into seven vibrations or frequencies:

The Mental Plane

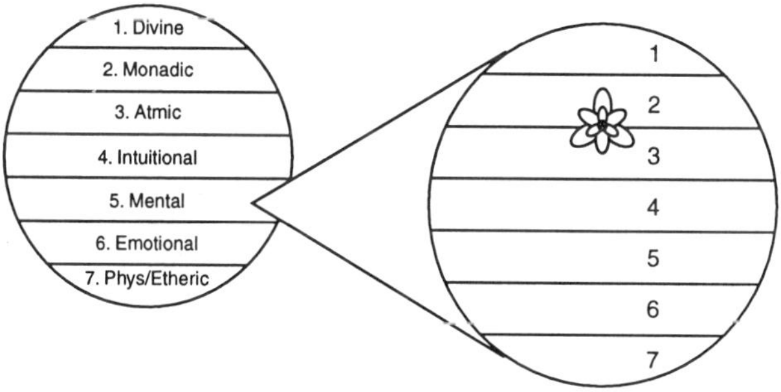

The seventh level of the mental plane is the densest level. The most subtle levels are the third, second, and first

1. See *The Subconscious Mind and the Chalice.*

levels. As you go toward higher levels in the mental plane, light increases.

The mental body is formed of millions of atoms. Each atom is a progressing light. The higher levels of the mental plane do not exist if the life does not first progress and create these levels. Every atom tries to evolve.

As your mental atoms graduate, your enlightenment and illumination increase and the mental body becomes radioactive and more powerful.

The seventh level is a very low mentality. As you develop your mental body, your sensitivity increases. Along with sensitivity, the power to be impressed increases. In other words, you become more sensitive to impression.

Nearly eighteen million years ago, the mental body of the human being, which was built of very low-level substance, was just a little cloud around the head of man.

At this stage man received no impressions or only very low-level impressions. He actually was half animal and half man. We are told that his suffering was so great that he cried out for help.

Our humanity consisted of failures from the moon. It seems that something drastic happened on the moon and our humanity was not able to finish its evolution there and graduate. The moon was destroyed and its humanity was brought to our planet.

The Planetary Life is a Great Mind, a Great Entity. The stars and planets are also the bodies of Great Beings. Even in ancient times, Zoroaster said that constellations were nothing else but the bodies of Great Beings Who graduated to a certain stage of evolution and built Their bodies in the skies.

One thing is evident: this planet has a mind. Every thing that grows here is arithmetical and geometrical; it has symmetry and a beginning and an end. This means that there is some conscious entity behind this planet or in this planet — even in every atom. Many scientists say that in the atom there is a great mind. Einstein once said that the deeper he thought and the farther he penetrated into the Universal Reality, the more obvious it became that there is a Great Mathematician behind all existence. There must be such a Mathematician — if we only had "eyes to see and ears to hear." To build an ear or an eye mechanically would take billions of dollars and five hundred scientists — and it would still be nothing compared to the real human ear or eye. What a Great Scientist is behind the creation of the human ear and eye — Whoever He is.

This Scientist or Architect is the Captain of this little spaceship we call Earth. The Captain felt that the little bugs called human beings were in danger, so according to the Ageless Wisdom He sent a call to space, to different solar systems, and one hundred and five very advanced Beings called Kumaras came to this planet as volunteers to help humanity to advance. Along with Them came millions of angelic Beings — the Solar Angels. These advanced Beings lived among men and even married with them to make humanity advance. In various scriptures this period is described as the time when gods walked among men.

Angels do not really have wings or human form. According to the Ageless Wisdom, an angel is an electrical wave, a wavelength, a spark. But because of our emotions and reactions, we give them form. We are the ones who give them form.

It is not the size of something that makes it exist. A Solar Angel is so small that It can sit on a mustard seed. The spirit of man is like a flashing arrow; it does not have a form. But because of our religious traditions, prejudices, and superstitions, we are cemented in our body consciousness and even think of God as a fat man sitting around with a pipe in His mouth, deciding whether the people who come before Him should be sent to heaven or to hell. In a sense, Michelangelo did a great disservice to humanity by portraying God in human form with such skill and artistry. And when we read that God created man in His own Image, we think that His Image has eyes, a nose, hands, and so on. These ideas are not found in the Ageless Wisdom. They are part of popular religion so that people act and behave in dignity.

The arrival of the Kumaras and millions of Angels to earth demonstrated a great law in the Universe: the Law of Sacrifice. There is no progress, no creation, no achievement in the world except through the Law of Sacrifice.

The Kumaras and Angels knew this law, and according to it the Angels said, "We will sacrifice ourselves and live with humanity until it is liberated." The first wave of Angels arrived and attempted to reach humanity, but humanity could not see or feel Them, and could not be impressed by Them through their minds because the minds of human beings had not yet developed. This wave of Angels eventually left humanity.[2]

2. See *Cosmos in Man*, pp. 25-31.

A second wave of Angels arrived two million years later. Before this wave arrived, humanity lived like animals for two million years on this planet. They could not progress. In order to help humanity, the second wave placed a spark of light in the minds of human beings to help them realize that they were not animals, and then these Angels left our planet. The spark that They placed is referred to in the New Testament in the parable of the woman who had three measures of flour to which she added leaven. These "measures" were the physical, emotional, and mental bodies of man, to which a spark of "leaven" — or light — was added.

This spark is a radioactive element that was placed in the mental body to make it responsive to a certain degree. Humanity needed something to speed its progress so that it could keep pace with the progress of the stars, galaxies, and the rest of the Universe. Humanity's slow progress was throwing the whole solar system out of balance.

One of the laws that governs the solar system is the Law of Attraction and Repulsion. This law is also called the Law of Equilibrium. If you are balanced between elements that you attract and repulse, you are in equilibrium. According to the Law of Attraction and Repulsion, a planet must receive energy and then repulse with a similar amount of energy so that the equilibrium of the solar system is maintained. When we receive less energy and release more energy, we put our planet in imbalance. Once this planet becomes imbalanced, the whole solar system is imbalanced. Many solar systems disappear from space because something went wrong on one of the planets. A great Sage says that if this planet creates too great an imbalance in the solar system, the Great Ones will take it out of the chain and replace it with another planet. This would be catastrophic for the human race.[3]

The third wave of Angels came two million years after the second wave. They saw that humanity was ready, so They entered into the mental bodies of human beings. The Angel within man is sometimes called the Guardian Angel, as explained in fairy tales. It actually exists. Some psychologists refer to this Inner Presence as the superconsciousness.

The Solar Angel descended into the third level of the mental plane, and like a mother It embraced the human soul. The human soul was like a spark in the bosom of the Solar Angel. The Solar Angel's body is like a bud with twelve inherent petals. It takes centuries for this bud to open, but when it opens it becomes a twelve-petaled Lotus. The Lotus is also called the Chalice, and it has twelve electrical energies.

The Solar Angel's radioactivity organized the physical, emotional, and mental bodies of man. Its energy worked like a magnet to put the physical, emotional, mental, and spiritual atoms into shape. St. Peter called the Solar Angel, "Christ within you, the hope of glory." This phrase is not referring to Christ, but to the One who changes you from within. Christ is the Solar Angel of all humanity, just as a Solar Angel serves an individual.[4]

Humanity is now progressing. Many people are in contact with their Solar Angels. This is the meaning of the advice found in the Ageless Wisdom which says that you must come in contact with your Inner Being, and that if you do

3. See Ch. 115, "Glory," in *The Psyche and Psychism.*
4. Agni Yoga Society, *Infinity*, Vol. 2, para. 226.

not come in contact with It, you are still walking in darkness.

The mental plane is like a ladder. When you are at the bottom, the whole world is very limited. When you climb a little higher up on the ladder, the world expands for you. As you continue up the ladder, the world is seen from a different perspective, your consciousness expands, and you become more sensitive.

The petals of the Lotus are like tongues of flame that have beautiful colors. As each petal opens, it brings to you corresponding energies from the petals of the planet, the solar system, and the galaxy.

In the fourth level of the mental plane, the mental unit is the automatic coordinator of the physical, emotional, and lower mental bodies. It is like a switch that automatically works to control these systems.

Each petal of the Lotus is a subtle mechanism that, when unfolded, provides psychic powers in man until that time when the human soul enters the Spiritual Triad. The outer nine petals develop the etheric, astral, and mental psychic powers. The three innermost petals bring in Triadal sensitivity, or higher psychic powers.

Solar Angels inspire us. They say to us, "Human children, look how beautiful and great We are. Progress exists within you. Rise and try to enter a higher level of existence." As you develop, the Solar Angel appears to you even more beautiful and Cosmic. This creates the urge in you to venture deeper. A time comes when you really can communicate with It; you ask questions and you receive revelations.

Until you clean yourself of inertia, glamor, and illusion, you will not be able to contact the Solar Angel directly. If your telephone line is obscured, you have static instead of clear communication. The human aura is filled with static, and unless the person cleans up, he cannot contact the Solar Angel.

If a person is an aspirant, one who is not lost in animal-like existence, he has three tasks. He must purify, discipline, and transmute his threefold lower nature. Purification means physical purification as well as the elimination of all separatism, hatred, jealousy, and negative emotions, and the development of the ability to think only right and beautiful thoughts.

The human being must strive to develop knowledge of himself. The causal body can be built with good deeds, good thoughts, and good aspiration. Aspiration brings buddhic energy to you. Service brings energy from the Atmic Plane. Sacrifice brings energy to you from the Divine Plane. Once the Sage D.K. said that service is greater than meditation. Service in this sense means labor performed for others without self-interest. How many human beings can do this? This kind of service is very rare.

The number of great Teachers is very few. Initiates and those who build inner contact are also rare. We are just like buds that are going to open into flowers, but millions of people are still closed. Who is going to open these buds? We live from one war to the next, from one exploitation to another, from one form of materialism to another — like mice running in the wheel of their cage.

The Lotus, or the causal body, contains three permanent atoms, which act like genes. From the physical-etheric permanent atom, the physical and etheric bodies are inherited. There is an astral permanent atom, which is like astral genes, and the mental permanent atom. Permanent atoms cause you to be born and bloom according to the actions performed in previous lives. If you worked very hard and your permanent atoms registered forty-five percent progress, you will incarnate with a physical body that has a forty-five percent ability to resist disease and weakness.

The three lower bodies must develop harmoniously if a person wants to live a long and happy life. If only one body is cared for, imbalance results. The health of the body is equal to its transformation. A person can physically live for ninety years like an animal, but when his astral and mental bodies develop, they exercise great pressure on the undeveloped body and create disturbances in it unless it develops along with the subtler bodies.

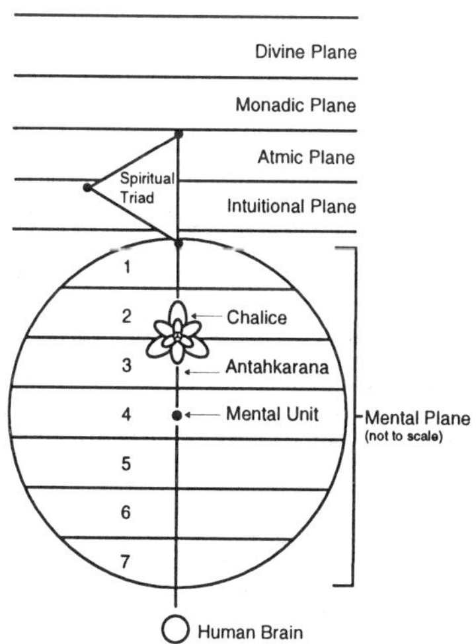

In the above diagram, the Spiritual Triad is called the Triangle of Fire. The Antahkarana, the Golden Bridge, or the Rainbow Bridge extends between the higher and the lower minds, between the mental unit and the mental permanent atom. This is the Bridge that must be built. You do not have a higher mind if you have not built this Bridge, which is constructed through meditation and service.

The Chalice is the body of the Solar Angel. In the center of the Chalice is the Spark, or human Monad. The Solar Angel tries to come into contact with the human being through meditation with certain vibrations, inspirations, and dreams. Millions of years ago, the Solar Angel contacted the human being through his dreams and instructed him, gave him advice, led him, and saved him from danger through dreams. Today the Solar Angel still communicates with the average person in his dreams.

Once you start functioning in the third, second, and first levels of the mental plane, you are no longer average. From this time on you are in direct contact with the Solar Angel. First you start hearing Its voice; then you see Its radiation. Finally, you see Its face, although this face has been created by your imagination because the human being comprehends existence through form. At this stage you see Its light like a diamond-colored spark when you close your eyes. The diamond may even be a little black. Slowly it becomes bigger and bigger and eventually hollow, like an eye. You then see a greater light. This is the meaning of the words of Christ, "We will see the light in a greater light." There will be three greater lights: the light of the Solar Angel, the radiation of the Chalice, and the Spark.

In *Infinity II*[4] we read, "The creative impulse impels the spirit to the Cosmic Magnet." The Cosmic Magnet is Almighty God, the center of creation. "The creative impulse gives birth to all strivings." Striving is the effort a person makes to become something higher, something more beautiful and more creative than his current state. "The creative impulse evokes from space the manifestations of cosmic rays." As a person strives, he reaches higher, and as he makes contact with the Cosmic Magnet, he becomes magnetic and draws to himself Cosmic energies from various sources. "Certainly, only a fiery spirit can sense all the forces needed for creativity...." The creative centers of advanced people collect the rays of space. The petals of their centers open like antennae and make them sensitive to Cosmic energies. These Cosmic energies are energies that flow, among others, from Sagittarius, Taurus, Aries, the Great Bear, the Pleiades, and Sirius. At this stage, most of us do not have the mechanism for recording these energies, but as we advance and the petals of our centers begin to open, we become the recipients of these energies.

With these energies we become geniuses, heroes, and leaders; we become more creative and we come in contact with Higher Worlds. As these energies flow into us, our contact with the Universe and with the Cosmos becomes more open and clear. Instead of feeling that we are lost human beings, that we are going to die, and that everything will end, we become Cosmic-conscious. Through this process, we come in contact with our Inner Being and we affirm with our own experience that an Immortal Being exists within

4. Agni Yoga Society, *Infinity, Vol. 2,* para. 226.

us. "Thus, the striving attracts the cosmic rays. Thus, We affirm the Chalice of the Agni Yogi to be a mighty treasury."

If you are acting in the causal plane, first of all you are very impersonal and do not involve yourself in personality reactions. You see things as clearly as possible from various viewpoints. You see your unity with other people and other viewpoints.

The twelve-petaled Lotus is composed of three love petals, three knowledge petals, and three sacrifice petals, with the human soul at their center. Each petal penetrates into a different body. For example, the first knowledge petal penetrates into the physical body, the second knowledge petal penetrates into the astral body, and the third knowledge petal penetrates into the mental body. When the knowledge petals open, we have physical, emotional, and mental knowledge.

The Lotus

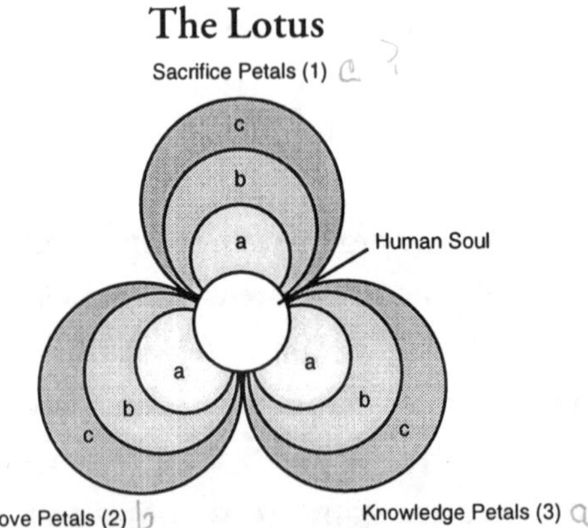

The love petals work in the same way. The first petal opens and penetrates into the physical body and creates physical love. The second petal opens and creates emotional love, and so on. Then sacrifice begins. When the sacrifice petal starts to open in the etheric body, you sacrifice everything physical. When it starts to open in the emotional body, you sacrifice everything emotional. When it opens in your mental body, you make yourself a living sacrifice.

Every time a petal opens, a planetary, solar, galactic, or Cosmic energy starts to flow into you, expanding your horizons so much that the values of your life change. When your standard of value changes, your actions and viewpoints change accordingly. For example, once a man owned a precious diamond for which he killed and exploited people. One day when he was stranded in the desert, very hungry and thirsty, he saw a man and offered to trade the diamond for food and water. He did not care about the precious diamond anymore because he could not eat or drink it in the desert. In the desert, a piece of bread and a cup of water became equal in value to the diamond.

The Lotus is also called the Chalice because in this "cup" is accumulated all that is beautiful, good, and truthful in our lives. All the physical, emotional, and mental jewels that we ever expressed are stored there. Any true act of knowledge, love, or sacrifice accumulates in the Chalice. Christ was referring to the Chalice when He said, "Don't keep your treasure in a bank where an enemy can penetrate." Worldly banks will sink into the ocean if an earthquake or other natural catastrophe occurs. There is only one safe place for your inner treasures: the Chalice. In reference to the Chalice, Christ also said,

"But lay up for yourselves a treasure in heaven, where neither rust nor moth destroy, and where thieves do not break through and steal. For where your treasure is, there also is your heart."[5]

and:

"Every scribe who is converted to the kingdom of heaven is like a man who is a householder, who brings out new and old things from his treasures."[6]

The treasury becomes richer and richer as you increase in true knowledge, when you exercise more love and light, and when you offer yourself as a sacrifice to humanity. The petals open very gradually. This process is related to initiation or expansion of consciousness.

The petals unfold according to the Ray of the Monad:

"For instance, if the Ray of the Monad is the Second Ray, the knowledge petal will be the first to open, but the second petal of love will almost parallel its development, being for that particular type of Ego the line of easiest unfoldment; the knowledge petal will be for it the most difficult to open."[7]

To understand this paragraph, we must study the following tabulation:

1. Sacrifice Petals
   - sacrifice .... S
   - love L
   - knowledge .... K

2. Love Petals
   - sacrifice .... S
   - love L
   - knowledge .... K

5. Matt. 6:20-21.
6. Matt. 13:52.
7. Alice A. Bailey, *A Treatise on Cosmic Fire*, p. 546.

3. Knowledge Petals
   - sacrifice .... S
   - love L
   - knowledge .... K

When the Monad is Second Ray, the knowledge petal of the Love Petals (2K) will open and the love petal (2L) will have a parallel development. But the Knowledge Petals (3SLK) will be the most difficult to open.

The innermost last three petals, which make up the twelve petals of the Chalice, can be called the Golden Case of the Jewel.

Every person has his Chalice; every nation has its Chalice, if the Lord of the World sanctions it. Every planet and solar system has its Chalice. All Chalices are related to each other. If a person's Chalice is open and unfolded, it brings a great amount of energy and wisdom from other Chalices.

"These nine petals are of a predominant orange hue, though the six other colors are found as secondary colours in a varying degree. The inner three petals are of a lovely lemon-yellow hue."[8]

The colors of the individual petals are given as follows. The first Knowledge petal is orange, green, and violet. The second Knowledge petal is orange, rose, and blue. The third Knowledge petal is orange, yellow, and indigo.

The first Love petal is rose, orange, green, and violet. The second Love petal is orange, rose, and blue. The third Love petal is rose, orange, yellow, and indigo.

The first Sacrifice petal is yellow, orange, green, violet, and rose. The second Sacrifice petal is yellow, orange, violet,

8. *Ibid.*, p. 762.

rose, and blue. The third Sacrifice petal is yellow, orange, rose, blue, and indigo.[9]

On the planetary-human level, the petals are called

1st *petal of civilization*
2nd *petal of culture*
3rd *petal of illumination*
4th *petal of cooperation*
5th *petal of loving understanding*
6th *petal of group-conscious love*
7th *petal of participation and sharing*
8th *petal of purpose*
9th *petal of creative precipitation and radioactivity*

The Self, or Monad, is at the center of the Lotus, but as yet It does not function; It is closed. Only the reflection of the Monad works in the physical, emotional, and mental planes. Until the Fourth Initiation you are not a soul; you are under the influence of many different impressions until the Fourth Initiation, when you are "born again." To be "born again" means that you now know that you are a human being, as well as a spiritual being.

The aspirant must purify, discipline, and transmute his threefold nature by taking the energy of light, love, and power and working on the physical body, guarding his mouth, and controlling his feelings and thoughts. Second, he must develop knowledge and educate himself, equipping his mental body with knowledge and expanding his consciousness by trying to be something higher than he is.

9. *Ibid.*, pp. 822-824.

When the Chalice starts to unfold and expand, it puts man in contact with Higher Worlds and it translates impressions coming from Higher Worlds in terms of human interest. The Chalice is our Temple; it is here where God and man dwell together.

The Solar Chalice is composed of millions of atoms. Each one is a Cosmic Initiate of varying degrees according to the unfoldment of the petals and its location in the Chalice.

The petals of the Solar Chalice spread hundreds of miles out of the solar system. This means that they penetrate the Cosmic Physical, Cosmic Astral, and Cosmic Mental Planes in which these Cosmic Initiates are active.

These Initiates are not from the second solar system, but They have been brought by our Solar Logos from the previous solar system as His Co-workers to lead to perfection all the Sparks living in the sphere of the solar system.

Glory to Thee!

Note: See also *The Subconscious Mind and the Chalice* for further details regarding the Chalice.

18

Individualization

The Solar Angel is not the human soul. The Solar Angel leaves the man at the Fourth Initiation, and man becomes an Arhat. If the Solar Angel were the human soul, then could an Arhat exist without a soul?

The Solar Angel is an Initiate of all degrees. The human soul is trying to pass each level one by one, at each initiation, with all his strivings and sacrifices.

Before the Solar Angels came, man was hovered over by the Monad. He had a Monad. Man was the Monad. But this Monad was not an individuality. It was a Ray activating the human vehicles by Its power. It had no mind and absolutely no individual characteristics. The Solar Angel came to create a womb for this Ray and individualize him.

When the Solar Angel builds the Chalice, the effulgent Ray of the Monad is conceived in this womb as the seed of the future human soul. And the seed of the Ray begins to develop intelligence, intelligent love, and intelligent power.

This is how the embryo of the future human soul comes into being. The maturation of this human soul will continue until the Fourth Initiation, after which the man will be a free human soul and lead his destiny by his own hands.

The Solar Angel will go do Its own business after accomplishing Its duty — the conception of the human soul, and its preparations for total individualization.

Remember that man existed before the advent of Solar Angels, and will exist after the Solar Angels leave him.

On one planet, the individualization did not take place by the help of Solar Angels. These individualized human beings did not need Solar Angels.

The real meaning of individualization is as follows:

The spiritual Monad is One, universal, boundless Ray. This Ray is the absolute. The Solar Angel takes it in, separates it from the whole, and makes it to develop the "I am consciousness." This is individualization.

There are many kinds of individualizations. We have physical, astral, and mental. We have individualization at the Third, Fourth, Fifth, and Sixth Initiations. We have individualization at the Seventh, Eighth, and Ninth Initiations.

In these individualizations the human soul takes control of the bodies by focusing his consciousness in the bodies he controls.

For example, most of us are not individualized in the astral body. We cannot yet use our astral body as we use our physical body. We do not have awareness of self in the astral body. The same is true about our mental, intuitional, and higher bodies.

As we advanced in our physical life after we were individualized in our physical existences, similarly we will record great progress in the higher domains when we individualize in astral and mental bodies, or in the higher bodies. Actually, the initiation process is a kind of individualization —

knowing and becoming yourself in higher bodies and in higher spheres.

Remember the goal of our lives on earth is to develop consciousness in all seven planes. When this is achieved we can say that man is individualized in the Cosmic Physical Plane by developing self-consciousness upon all three seven subplanes.

There are three major individualizations:

1. The first one is the individualization of personality — "I am."
2. The second one is the individualization of the soul — "I am that."
3. The third one is the individualization of the Self — "I am that I am." which is achieved in the Spiritual Triad.

All these individualization processes must be actualized as

1. individuals
2. groups
3. nations
4. humanity

The drama of initiations must be played on all these domains. This is how the Cosmic Magnet functions and creates responses to the Its Rays.

Every Monad at the beginning was "I am that I am" but without consciousness. The individualization process is the awakening and the knowing that the Monad was the whole, and now It is the whole with a completed consciousness.

19

Cooperation in Light

A person who is growing in soul-consciousness begins to discard his ego and vanity and starts to cooperate in the Light.

To cooperate means to join efforts, skills, and labor for a common goal in the same plan. If you are cooperating as a group, everyone in that group combine all their skills, labors, and efforts to do something, to achieve something. Where there is harmony between efforts, skills, and labor, there exists cooperation.

In the Bible there is an example of cooperation. People came together and planned to build the Tower of Babylon. The construction went on very well in the beginning. People were really cooperating to build the Tower. But at some point, some turbulence occurred in their psyche and they did not want to cooperate with each other anymore, and the Tower was not completed.

The Tower of Babylon exists everywhere. When, in any work, people stop cooperating with each other, the Tower will not reach completion. People may begin to build a Tower, but then some parts of their nature do not cooperate and the Tower remains half built.

If your body, emotions and mind cooperate with your visions, ideas, and soul, you can accomplish great works and you will become a Tower in your nation and in humanity.

When people have cooperation within themselves, you can see it in their walk, speech, writing, or in their artistic expression. The most impressive art, or any other expression, is the one which contains a spirit of cooperation.

One day my Teacher analyzed in front of us a poem in which there was no harmony, no cooperation. He said, "These ideas do not have cooperation. The expressions do not have cooperation with the ideas. The expressions and ideas do not cooperate with the vision."

Any absence of cooperation in our labor and expression cannot have a strong impact upon people. Disunity in any form is lack of cooperation. There is power in cooperation; there is beauty and joy in cooperation.

It is possible to measure the strength of individual people when they cooperate. Let us say that to lift a log and put it onto a truck takes two horse power. But if you have three men each with one-half horse power, and if they cooperate, they will be able to lift the log.

One may ask, "From where did we gain the extra one-half horse power of energy?" The answer is that cooperation multiplies energy. You will find out that when these three men cooperate, they will produce the two horse power required to move the log.

The same phenomenon is true for those who cooperate with their emotions, thoughts, ideas and visions. Every act of cooperation multiplies energy.

Cooperation kindles your energy centers and stimulates them. That is why when you cooperate with a few people, you feel a strong sensation which has not yet been defined.

People think if they cooperate, they will lose something and they do not want to lose anything. They do lose something — their ego and self-interest — but in truth, they gain. They gain in losing their ego, and gain in raising the prosperity of a group of people. In cooperation, you increase. If you do not cooperate, you decrease.

That is the symbol of the Tower. When people cooperated, the height of the Tower increased. When they fought against each other, the Tower stopped growing and began to disintegrate. When there is cooperation, a family, a group, a nation grows. Without cooperation, all slowly disintegrates.

There is no true cooperation if the parties involved are not striving toward creating better conditions in life to promote transformation of life, expansion of consciousness, greater creativity, health, and happiness.

Murderers can collaborate and their collaboration cannot be called cooperation. In cooperation there is something sacred, transcendent, beautiful, which is directed toward synthesis.

Collaboration can be in any direction, for any reason. Cooperation is the synchronization of hearts and souls and, of course, the harmonization of actions and directions.

Collaboration exists on the mental and physical planes. Beyond that, it turns into cooperation. Cooperation has always carried with it the light of Beauty, Goodness, Righteousness, Joy, Freedom, Striving, and Sacrificial Service.

If "cooperation" is carried out under the pressure of selfish, separative interests, it can be called collaboration but not real cooperation. In every cooperative labor shines the flame of love and sacrifice, solemnity and perseverance, endurance and balance. Great is the beauty of the spirit of cooperation.

Cooperation is possible only when the individuals have the same vision or the same purpose. If the vision or the purpose is not the same, then there will be no cooperation. If the vision is the same, the vision itself will orchestrate all efforts, all labor, skills, and ideas and will create cooperation. The vision, or the purpose, of the cooperating members will charge each one of them with its fire and magnetism and will make people understand each other, respect each other, and cooperate with each other.

There are two major enemies within man. One is his ego; the other is vanity. It is known that the creative and constructive work of a group is not possible unless these two enemies in man are eradicated.

Many psychological techniques can be used to try and eliminate these enemies, but all such efforts end with failure. There is only one way to eliminate such enemies, and that is through the process of cooperation.

In a school where I was the director, there were certain students with big egos and lots of vanity. I put them in with those teams that were highly cooperative in certain labors. When they first joined, they created many problems. But slowly the team absorbed them, annihilating their ego and vanity, exposing to them their true worth in any given job.

A boy who once had lots of ego came to me and said very sincerely, "I thought I was something and that I could do almost everything. Working with these fellows showed me how unskilled I was and how much vanity I had. Thank you for helping me see my real self."

If you want to cure yourself of ego and vanity, try cooperation. Try to obey the boss. Try to obey the rules and regulations. Try to cooperate with everyone on the team.

It is interesting that cooperation builds sensitivity in us to see the common purpose and it unites our efforts with others to actualize that purpose. We also feel that actualizing a common purpose is not against our individual interest but for it.

Ten people who lived in the same village individually tried to build a lake by a river, but each one failed. They finally formed a group to create the lake. Successful in cooperating with each other, they now share the beautiful lake in many ways.

One day, when my Father and I were sitting by the river, he said, "Bring me two rocks from the river." I brought him two rocks, one shaped like a ball and another with sharp edges. After looking at the rocks for a while, he asked, "Which of these rocks has traveled the longest road? You do not need to answer instantly. When the answer comes to your mind, come and tell me."

After playing half an hour, I had the answer. "Father," I said, "this round one traveled the longer road." "Why do you think that?" he asked. "Because it became round by hitting the other rocks as it traveled down the stream and as it became rounder, it traveled faster." "I like that," he said.

"That is how it became a ball — by touching other rocks, by cooperating with the tide or the flow of the river. Can you imagine how the other rocks helped this rock to become a round ball? Its squareness disappeared as it rolled and created friction with all the other rocks."

After pausing a while, he added, "The rock had an ego and the ego told the rock, 'Do not move; stay where you are.' But when the rain came, it was swept into the river, and it wanted to cooperate with the currents. This is like those who eliminate their ego and vanity and enter into the tide of cooperation."

People will remain "square" until they learn how to cooperate.

A cooperative person has multidimensional talent to fit in groups and cooperate with them. But "squares" — those who are filled with ego and vanity — do not fit and do not develop. The best way to make such people develop is to pull them slowly into greater and greater cooperative labors.

It is interesting to see that neither religion nor education can help you remove ego and vanity. As a matter of fact, vanity and ego can be seen in abundance in those who are devoted to certain religions, or in those who have graduated from certain universities. These institutions build such vanity and ego in people that when they face life they feel hurt every moment and see their inadequacies. Only by cooperation in life problems can one slowly leave behind his ego and vanity, because life gradually strips the false self from them.

Ego and vanity limit your expansion, your consciousness, your wisdom. As you get rid of them, you feel the expansion of your consciousness, understanding, and lovingness.

Cooperation must start at home from childhood. Our homes are schools where we can learn the fundamentals of cooperation. A cooperating family is a happy, healthy, prosperous, and creative family. When cooperation stops in the family, pain, suffering, and various problems enter. This is true also in our factories and offices, in any kind of organized labor. Where there is cooperation, there is great success and great satisfaction. To cooperate, we harmonize ourselves with others.

Our evolution, our refinement is subject to our cooperation. The best symbol of cooperation is an orchestra. The greater the cooperation between the musicians, the greater will be the influence of their music on the audience.

The art of cooperation is not only found on the physical level. There are many dimensions of cooperation. We can cooperate on the physical, emotional, mental, and spiritual levels. The higher our level of cooperation, the greater is our success and our impact on others. Five hundred people who cooperate with their muscles can move a mountain. But if those people cooperate emotionally and mentally, they can move nations. If they cooperate on all levels, they can move humanity toward a new dimension. The higher the cooperation, the greater the results.

Higher cooperation evokes the light that is hidden within our cells, atoms, centers, and soul, and we walk on the path of illumination by exercising fourfold cooperation. The ability to cooperate indicates that you have no ego, no vanity, no wounds, and no negative associations in your consciousness. It means that you have overcome them through service, labor, and cooperation.

You can see such beautiful people in great fields of labor who are embodiments of cooperation. Cooperation develops intuitive understanding. After a long life of cooperation, people understand each other without words. They all do their job without even a command. They meet each other's need without a request. Intuition develops to such a degree that the members of a cooperative group act as if they are one organism.

Once I visited a friend's home for dinner. After dinner, his wife asked their daughter if she would help wash the dishes. To my amazement, the seventeen-year-old daughter made an ugly gesture and said, "Mom, I have to watch a program on TV," and ran to her room. The wife worked very hard. When the program was over, the girl came back to the living room. As the others were engaged in a heated discussion, I called the girl to me, put my arm around her, and said, "If I ask you five questions, will you give me five really honest answers?" "Why not?" she giggled.

"The first question is, how many months did your mother carry you in her womb?"

"Nine months."

"Good. And how many months did she breast-feed you?"

"I think fourteen months."

"Good. Now the third question. How many years did she clean your clothes, your sheets, and so on?"

"Almost seventeen."

"Good. The fourth question is, how many years has your mother cooked for you, fed you, and clothed you?"

"Almost seventeen."

"Good. The last question is, how have you expressed gratitude to her for all her labor?"

She looked in my eyes and kept silent. Then she said, "Good night," and disappeared to her room.

Because I knew the family, I kept track of her life. She dropped out of school, left the family, went to work as a bartender, and came home drunk every night.

Those who have no gratitude cannot cooperate. Without gratitude and cooperation, they become losers in life. Life grinds people until their vanity and ego are exhausted. But this is carried out through long periods of suffering and pain.

When we say, "cooperation in light," what do we really mean? People cooperate in crime, in terrorism, in exploitation, in manipulation, and in suppressing people. Such cooperation is cooperation in darkness and for darkness. But cooperation in light is different.

Light is a state of consciousness in which you can see what it is you really are, what others really are, and what the highest good for all of us really is. We see further how this highest good can be brought in for all of us.

When such a light hits you, when your consciousness reaches such a level, you begin to walk the path of cooperation and, with the help of others, you bring health, happiness, and prosperity to all concerned.

Further cooperation in light means to cooperate to promote Beauty, Goodness, Righteousness, Joy, Freedom, Gratitude, and Striving.

Cooperation is possible only if

1. You know what you are
2. You know what your co-workers are
3. You know what the Common Good is

Cooperation in darkness is cooperation for selfish interest, separatism, exploitation, and greed. Cooperation in light means cooperation with those who are enlightened, honest, noble, full of higher ideas and visions. If your consciousness is in darkness and you are imprisoned in ignorance, there is little chance that you can cooperate consciously.

It is interesting that simple people cooperate with each other if they have a good leader, and they accomplish good things. This is because their ego is not yet built, and they are not eager to use people for their ego or vanity.

Average people, those who build their egos, cooperate for their self-interests to meet their wants and needs. People who are sophisticated in education work together only when they are in danger. They work against an enemy, against a group, against an authority to protect their interests or rights. Such people cannot really cooperate because their egos and vanities are strongly built. Their pretended cooperation is based only on self-interest. They impose themselves upon others; they violate the rights and freedoms of others, often in the name of cooperation.

A true disciple is one who truly and continually cooperates with others because of his dedication to the Teacher, Who symbolizes the Plan and Purpose of life. Highest cooperation is possible only within the groups of Initiates and the Hierarchy.

The word "Hierarchy" esoterically stands for harmony and conscious cooperation. M.M. says, "One must hear Our singing in order to understand the life of Our Ashrams."

They cooperate because They know what the Purpose and Plan are. They cooperate because throughout ages They traveled the long path of sacrifice and service. They exist only to make the Plan and Purpose manifest.

Unless one exists only for a great purpose, he cannot fully cooperate. Cooperation is possible only when you have vision and are identified with that vision to such a degree that your little self is totally lost in its light. Cooperation in light is possible only through self-forgetfulness.

A person who constantly thinks of his own interests, money, vacations, comforts, pleasures, and luxuries will never reach a state of consciousness in which he can cooperate.

A beehive is the symbol of cooperation. Discipleship groups must be like beehives. The Hierarchy is the supreme example of cooperation because each Great One is inspired by the Light of Christ.

Those who cooperate in light are those who live in light, who live and work in such a way that they do not hurt the goal toward which they work. When our light increases, our cooperative efforts increase. As our consciousness expands, our cooperation becomes better and better. As our consciousness dims, our cooperation fails.

Every growing, blooming, and maturing flower, tree, animal, or man is a symbol of cooperation. The symbol of disunity and disintegration is a corpse.

Among those things that work against cooperation are

- fear
- anger
- jealousy
- selfishness
- greed
- ego
- malice
- slander
- gossip
- treason
- hatred
- vanity

These create short circuits in any cooperative system.

When your light increases, you see the hindrances in you, and unless you eliminate them you cannot become a co-worker of Light. There are many psychological hindrances within us, that prevent cooperation. They can be our glamors, posthypnotic suggestions, and so on. Whatever they are, they surface when we sincerely try to cooperate. And it is only in the process of trying to cooperate that we drop our hindrances and clear our way.

To cooperate with Higher Forces is the greatest honor for a person, but such cooperation comes on our path only if we prepare ourselves, increase our skills, and destroy our vanities and ego.

Any effort to cooperate with a group of people brings to the surface of your consciousness all those elements that hinder your cooperation. And through your efforts you can eliminate them.

It is easy to be a holy person in retreat, but it is difficult to be a holy person in a group of people who are loaded with problems and vanities. It is such a state of relationship that draws out of a person's nature many characteristics about which the person is totally unaware. This gives the person an opportunity to eliminate those elements.

Our weaknesses also appear when we have just been promoted to a higher office. Our vanity and ego surface and gradually bring us down to the common level where we were before or make us a pain in the life of those who work under us.

Before one learns true cooperation, he must clean many hindrances from his nature. A person can do this if he catches himself in moments when he finds that he is being uncooperative. He must then ask himself, "What is it in me that is preventing me from cooperating?"

Those who want to cooperate must develop skills that will assist them to become more efficient workers. They must cultivate virtues to keep their skills from blocking their progress.

The higher you go on the scale of cooperation, the higher your skills must be. But skills without virtue can be used for self-interest or for destructive purposes. The cultivation of virtue makes your skills more useful, acceptable, and also keeps you humble and progressive.

Those people who want to cooperate protect each other. They do not hurt or cut each other. On the contrary, they help each other and care for each other.

Unless those who cooperate help and protect each other, cooperation will be impossible because destructive forces will scatter them and make each of them useless.

Our cooperation increases in its efficiency as we care for each other. People who really cooperate are tested in risky, dangerous jobs, where the job requires self-forgetfulness and self-sacrifice.

In ancient times kings used to select their immediate co-workers from those soldiers who used to risk their life to cooperate with the commander during the most dangerous missions. Real co-workers emerge during the time of danger.

It is easy to cooperate in parties and at gala dinners, but true co-workers emerge only in times of danger or turbulence. Generally, true co-workers do not talk about their heroic works to emphasize their personality. They individually take care of their own physical, emotional, and mental health so that they do not become stumbling blocks for others.

Five of us as young boys were escaping from a town where the government was killing the citizens. We were escaping through a mountain gorge and one of us was jumping from rock to rock as if he were having fun, instead of walking carefully. A few times we warned him to walk like a human being; he continued to play and so we walked ahead. He was still jumping carelessly when we heard him cry, "I broke my leg!" We were scared to death. We were trying to escape quickly, and here lay this boy, keeping us close to the town.

We rushed to him and tried to pull him up on our backs, but he was heavy — we were in panic and fear. Eventually, we tied him on a branch and pulled him through the gorge, waiting any minute for someone to come and kill us. Eventually we reached a safe place and looked down the gorge in time to see the murderers coming! They had just missed us.

If you want to cooperate with people, especially during critical times, do not break your "leg" so that you do not hamper the progress of others in their labor. Co-workers must take care of their physical bodies as well as their emotional and mental bodies. They must try to be up-to-date in order not to hinder the cooperative efforts of their co-workers.

Every group is an organism. The whole organism must progress. In discipleship groups, those who do not take care of their physical, emotional, and mental bodies turn into sources of problems for the group. Those who start their courses and do not finish them, but then find opportunities to work on committees, create problems because they do not understand their duties, responsibilities, or what work is expected of them.

I remember a person who came to work in one of our offices who had a cold. One day I said to her, "I don't want you to come to my office until your cold is gone." The next month she came to my office. "Why do you hate me?" she asked. "I want to come and ask you some questions." "I do not hate you," I said, "but I do hate your cold. I don't want to catch a cold because it will interfere with my lectures and seminars." "I can't understand you," she said as she left my office.

Every month she had a cold, but she refused to go to the doctor and she did not take care of herself. I was forced to let her resign.

Cooperation is impossible without sensitivity and without taking care of your health. You must take care of yourself so that you do not become a burden to others and slow down their labor.

Each member of a nation, a group, or a family has a right to demand that the other members are healthy, prosperous, creative, and victorious. Only through such a demand can the sense of responsibility grow within us.

Such a demand must be a sincere expectation from the other members of the group to take care of themselves so as not to cause waste of time and energy or to spread headaches to others.

Those who have the spirit of cooperation unite with all those activities which try to bring health, happiness, prosperity, and enlightenment into the world. Eventually we will realize that we are part of a living organism and we cannot live for ourselves only.

Co-workers never encourage weakness, stupidity, treason, or vices. They do not flatter these traits in others because they see in them a great danger of degeneration.

Co-workers live under the direction of their soul, which is the light within. The soul stands for

- Discipline
- Labor
- Striving

If you are guided to exercise greater discipline, to labor and strive, then your guidance is from the right source. Follow such guidance.

Discipline is an effort to conquer the mechanical side of your being.

Labor is continuous effort to bring the highest out of you. The ancients said, "A tool that is used shines. A tool that is not used rusts."

Striving is a continuous effort to surpass your beingness.

The greatest enemy of people is one who flatters and makes them feel good about all the dirt they have in their nature. In cooperation, no flattery is acceptable.

Cooperation starts in thought. It is impossible for people to cooperate if their thoughts are not in harmony with each other. Thought can be harmonious if it is trained in the discipline of Beauty, Goodness, Righteousness, Joy, Freedom, Sacrificial Service, and Striving.

Average people cooperate under a leader. Sophisticated people, those with knowledge, fight with one another. Real disciples cooperate in the light of the Teacher. The Hierarchy is a symbol of cooperation in the light of the Plan.

Just as we tune our musical instruments, Masters tune Their disciples so that unanimously and simultaneously they can respond to Their impressions and directions. You cannot have a functional device if all parts of that device are not prepared to meet the purpose of the device.

Cooperation is impossible unless the ego and vanity are taken away. We are told that the Planetary Chalice is formed of Ninth Degree Initiates. The Solar Chalice is formed of Those Who have graduated from the Fifth Cosmic Initiation and have been trained to consciously fit Themselves for solar responsibilities.

All Their labor in the Cosmos is carried on by the Law of Cooperation. The Law of Cooperation and the Law of Sacrifice run parallel. No one can cooperate unless he develops, from his childhood, the spirit of sacrifice. In cooperation one learns to renounce things that are not necessary for the labor. Cooperation is carried on only through a person who is becoming more and more free.

Without sacrifice, no freedom is possible. Without sacrifice and freedom from former limitations, no cooperation is possible.

Cooperation is the royal path leading to the All Self.

20

Meditation and the Human Soul

Meditation is an effort to shift your consciousness from lower levels to the higher levels of mind. Meditation, in general, starts at the fourth level, the concrete level of the mind, and for a long time people stay at that level, feeling that they are doing right meditation. On the fourth level of mind, generally we try to analyze things, compare things, and try to find their qualities and relationships. But after a while, if we do not climb to the next level of mind, thinking becomes mechanical, self-centered, or boring, and slowly we wish to stop our meditation.

It is not easy to make a breakthrough into the third level of the mind, where we come in contact with the world of meaning and the essence of things we are meditating upon.

The concrete mind in a sense ties our feet to worldly interests, and we feel that if we enter into the abstract mind we lose our self-interest, factuality, and contact with the concrete world. There is also resistance from the third level of mind because it is a sphere of higher frequency, the speed is faster and forms are intangible in the hands of logic. Many people quit meditating when they feel such resistance.

One of my Teachers used to say that it is very difficult to cross into the third level of mind because of strong winds blowing across the bridge leading to the third level. Perhaps these winds are streams of energies coming from the Chalice, or they may be fiery waves testing the worthiness of the pilgrim trying to penetrate into the Higher Worlds. But those who persist in their meditation sooner or later make a breakthrough and penetrate into the world of meaning, vision, and cause.

Consciousness must penetrate into still higher levels of the mind until the highest level is achieved. It is here that the advanced Initiate drops the anchor of the ship of consciousness and makes it a base location of striving. But being able to focus our consciousness on the highest level of the mental plane will not lead us to a state of abstraction. Through meditation the network of communication is established with the lower mind and the pilgrim can, at will, use both parts of his mind to achieve balance: using the lower mind to contact the world of concrete values, problems, and needs of the world; and using the higher mind to shed light, love, and beauty upon the lower world to meet its problems.

When the communication network is completed, the whole mental plane works as a unit. Meditation helps to unify the mind and to build the communication network so that later, when the human soul penetrates into the Spiritual Triad, it can use the mental mechanism for its creative work.

Creativity is the ability to contact ideas, inspirations, visions, and impressions in the Spiritual Triad to formulate them into colors of beauty within the mental body and express them through words, formulas, sounds, colors, motions, and forms.

Those who penetrate into the abstract levels of mind demonstrate pure idealism while manifesting practicality in all their relationships and services. The world of values and the world of practical concrete forms become one world. This is why such people are true leaders. Practical life becomes chaotic if the light of abstract worlds does not illuminate it. Or, if a man is trapped in the Higher Worlds without being in clear contact with the lower world, he becomes a useless dreamer, lost in his visions.

It is important to know that the communication network built between the mental levels is not one kind of network. This network generally is built with mental substance, but in that mental substance there can exist strands of varying Ray energies: First Ray, Second Ray, Third Ray, and so on. As the network approaches completion, it becomes a Rainbow with the energies of all Seven Rays. The perfected Rainbow is a transmitter of Ray energies and related zodiacal energies. How powerful and abundantly creative is the person whose Rainbow is complete!

Meditation lays the foundation for the building of the Rainbow and carries on its construction to completion. The deeper, the more persistent is your meditation, the more soundly your Rainbow is built.

Communication lines increase year after year, life after life, until the mental plane, as a unified field of energy, turns into a central station of contact.

The mental body has many specialized centers which perform various jobs, such as receiving, assimilating, and translating the traffic of impressions coming from higher or lower realms. These specialized centers are related to specific neurons which act like programmed diskettes. The capacity of the "diskette" determines the creative manifestation of the mental currents.

Meditation not only builds specialized centers in the mental body, but it also builds and programs specialized groups of neurons or "diskettes" in the brain. The more evolved is the brain, the greater is its capacity to manifest accurately higher currents coming from mental centers.

Meditation, which helps the brain organize and fuse closer to the mental body, actually prepares a healthy future for man. Because it is the brain that manages the health of the body, the more organized the mind of man is, the greater is his probability of survival.

The brain is an independent organ in the sense that it continues to work, even if the mental body is suspended. The reason for this is that certain neurons are like automatic record/play-back machines. But the task of meditation is not only to bring the brain under the full control of the human soul via the mental body, but is also to erase certain "diskettes" which contain programs inherited from millions of years of living in the human or animal kingdoms.

Neurologists admit that it took approximately six hundred to seven hundred million years to construct our brain into the complicated masterpiece that it is.

The Rainbow Bridge

The Ageless Wisdom recognizes the existence of genes and DNA in the physical body. But it is also taught that there are similar recorders in the mental body which record all that has happened to a person from the time of his individualization. Further, the Ageless Wisdom states that all learning and experience are recorded in a "diskette" called the Chalice, and that the genes and DNA of the body operate according to the recordings made on these "diskettes."

Meditation, in building the Rainbow Bridge between the body, emotions, mental body, and Spiritual Triad, gives man an opportunity to bring forth recordings stored in deeper and higher sources which can change the contents of genes and DNA. This change is caused by energy currents, visualization, and creative imagination. It will one day be possible to form a body which will live as long as one wants by revitalizing the cells, neurons, genes, and DNA with advanced meditation. Meditation of this caliber even attacks viruses, microbes, and germs with the laser light of the human soul.

The brain is formed by those cells which, throughout millions of years, took initiations on higher levels of beingness and eventually formed the central nervous system of the body. These advanced and specialized neurons are embodiments of the recordings found in the permanent atoms and the Chalice projected onto specialized cells and neurons and actualized through the genes and DNA.

It is true that a new-born baby is affected by the genes and DNA of his parents. But he also has his own independent genes and DNA, as he carries the prototypes of these genes and DNA — his permanent atoms — life after life.

In the future when science penetrates into the complexity of genes and DNA, it will be able to discriminate between what are inherited recordings from parents and what are rolled-over recordings from past lives.

The future of humanity does not exist in medicine or in physics but in meditation, using visualization, creative imagination, and, in higher cases, through direct command, to create, to heal — or to destroy. Through meditation a person can introduce beneficent changes in his genes and DNA by contacting their prototypes — the permanent atoms — in the etheric, astral, and mental bodies.

A human soul advances, like any cell or neuron, through specializing himself so that he is suitable for greater and greater labor. A human soul can be a petal in an Ashramic flower; it can be an atom in the Chalice of a greater Entity. Specialization in the esoteric sense means to meet the demands and characteristics of your Monadic Ray.

The process of specialization is carried on through meditation. Through meditation, specialized cells and neurons are trained and drawn to their right locations. Through meditation, the human soul is specialized and drawn to the location where it will be of greatest service.

The promotion of a cell or neuron is controlled by the programming impressed upon the human soul. This programming continues until the person begins to live consciously — as a self-conscious soul — using his mechanisms as a separate unit. From this moment forward, the specialization process of his cells, neurons, and atoms comes under the conscious control of the human soul through meditation. Through meditation the lower atoms, cells, and neurons graduate, take initiations, and serve in greater capacity in the whole mechanism.

This is what we call the process of transmutation, transformation, and transfiguration as far as the personality is concerned. After that, the process of resurrection begins to penetrate into intuitional, atmic, and monadic levels and build the subtle mechanism through which the human soul contacts a greater universe.

Medicine, in general, is centered around chemistry and diet. But ideas, dreams, visions, hope, courage, daring, and heroism are also foods which create very special chemicals in our system. Meditation increases a pro-survival chemistry in our system. Through the intake of these special foods and the subsequent production of a pro-survival chemistry, many sicknesses and disease-producing factors are annihilated.

Space medicine is becoming a reality. Through meditation the human soul absorbs elements in space which are not composed of matter but are composed of mental or intuitional substances. By absorbing such elements through meditation, contemplation, and visualization, the human soul creates chemical compounds in the body which help the body survive in unbelievable conditions.

In the history of the Armenian church we read how a holy man was thrown into a dungeon. For fourteen years being denied physical food he lived only on "angel's food," the chemicals and elements received through meditation and prayer. When he was finally released, his body had become like a black charcoal, but he was physically fit and healthy. This man was the one who lead his nation to the Light of Christ.

By studying mystic and religious literature we find many similar examples of how meditation, prayer, aspiration, and sincere striving toward higher values keep the bodies alive — not food, chemicals, or doctors. Meditation will be the vanguard of the coming age.

Science discusses how light causes different effects when people use different prescriptions or chemicals. This, of course, is not too difficult to comprehend. But medical professors and scientists refuse to accept that light affects people who are occupied with negative thoughts and emotions differently than those who are occupied with positive thoughts, joy, and other positive emotions. This field must be researched in detail.

Sun rays and the rays of different sources of light have a different effect on those who are preoccupied with various thoughts and emotions. For example, sunlight is dangerous to those who are destructive, who think about exploitation and crime. This is why such people instinctively seek darkness. They haunt dark places and even wear sunglasses, avoiding contact with light because the light filtering through the layers of their evil thoughts and negative emotions produces various organic and nervous disorders or growths.

On the other hand, those who have lofty thoughts and emotions benefit from light because their pure thoughts and emotions digest light and use the chemistry of light as a source of nutrition. This is only one of the benefits received from meditation. A person who meditates also creates a thought layer and an emotional layer which filter out bad influences while allowing sunlight to heal, regenerate, and purify his system.

In the future those human beings who create such a "filter" or sphere around their bodies will survive when the ozone layer reaches a very dangerous depletion. Survival of the fittest means the survival of those who are agents of goodness and are full of joy, goodwill, and gratitude. Evil will destroy itself because the sphere it creates around itself is one which does not protect, but actually draws destructive rays of the sun or of light coming from various artificial sources.

It is important for people to learn to meditate and enrich their spheres with good thoughts, good emotions, and joy if they want to live a happier life.

All of this is possible through the science of meditation.

21

Charisma

A person has charisma when his psychic energy is in operation within and around him. Psychic energy is the energy of the human Core. When it is released, a person becomes a magnetic, radiating, influential, and efficient person who has the power to attract, heal, enlighten, and liberate people.

Psychic energy evokes devotion, dedication, and sacrifice from the hearts of other people. They feel uplifted and expanded in their consciousness. A charismatic person also evokes striving, courage, and daring from others. He increases the spirit of cooperation among people.

In the presence of a charismatic person, people feel as if their problems no longer create barriers on their path. They see light breaking through the clouds and miraculously enough, many of their questions are answered in the presence of a charismatic person.

The presence of a charismatic person liberates people's souls from the traps of glamors, illusions, and vanity. In his presence, they feel free from the prisons they once occupied.

All of this is accomplished through psychic energy, which radiates through the soul of a charismatic person and creates

- Beauty
- Goodness
- Righteousness
- Joy
- Freedom
- Unity
- Synthesis

Sometimes people think that certain people are charismatic when they demonstrate forceful influence upon others. In reality, such people do not have charisma but are channeling the force of some astral and dark entities through obsession or possession.

Entities, like huge magnets, create a field of magnetism around a person that they use as a device for destruction, corruption, and hatred. This field is sometimes misinterpreted as being charisma. An example of this was Hitler, who had the "charisma" to deceive and mislead an entire nation. Others were Enver Pasha and Sultan Hamid, who used their "charisma" to commit the mass genocide of Armenians.

True charisma is the effect of psychic energy. When psychic energy creates charisma, it leads the person toward greater creative, constructive actions, toward unity, health, happiness, prosperity, and enlightenment. Jesus had charisma. His whole intention was to liberate humanity.

Real charisma cannot be acquired through cosmetic or artificial decoration. Neither is it something that can be learned. It is the result of age-long striving for light, for beauty, and for service. It is not something that you can have — but something that you can be.

Schools that profess to teach charisma only tell you how to dress, how to talk, how to hide your motives, what gestures to use, how to answer questions, how to change your voice, and so on. They build artificial charisma which, like a cosmetic, disappears under the presence of stress and labor.

Real charisma begins the moment a person receives the fire of Spirit and turns into a huge magnet of wisdom, power, and fearlessness.

Real charisma is not a tool used to win elections, obtain money, reach high positions, or manipulate people. It is the intention of real charisma to bring greater beauty to life, greater joy and freedom to humanity. Everyone who is touched by the fire of charisma becomes a fiery servant of humanity.

It is important to remember that the dictionary definition of charisma is "a divinely conferred gift; a special spiritual power or personal quality that gives an individual influence or authority over large numbers of people."[1]

Of course, when one is gifted with psychic energy — with the Holy Spirit — he may still need to learn how to write, use the computer, or organize lectures and learn how to meet the needs of different levels of people because of the complex society in which we live. But remember that he already has fire. When he learns the ways to put his fire into

1. The Random House Dictionary.

motion, he becomes a flame that builds its own ways and means to kindle the hearts of the masses.

A true charismatic person can damage himself by using artificial means to appear authentic instead of being himself. I remember my Father speaking to a woodcarver. "Do not use that wood," my Father said to him. When the man asked, "Why?" my Father replied, "Because that wood will fall apart in two years. Use wood that will last for at least two decades." On the way home, my Father said to me, "One must have the right materials to produce something great. This applies also to people. When you work hard on a person who is spiritually worthless, you experience great disappointment."

Charisma is the magnetism that draws people to an individual who is charismatic. This magnetism can be the result of

1. the fire of enthusiasm
2. courage
3. psychic energy
4. vision
5. heroism, determination
6. beauty, grace
7. solemnity

Charisma is sometimes thought to be the result of

1. power
2. force
3. fixed intention
4. power of organization
5. manipulation

6. hypnotic influence
7. separatism

Both sets of qualities can create magnetism. One set is real and constructive; the other is false and destructive. Both sets are thought of as charismatic, but they are not. One attracts through spiritual magnetism while the other forces people into slavery.

Real charismatic people do not influence others merely because of their force, appearance, or position but through their psychic energy, beauty, ideas, visions, and sincerity.

Real charisma is not related to feelings and emotions. Real charisma can even shock us emotionally and wipe out our feelings. Real charisma is recognized not by emotions but by our intuition. We feel that the charismatic man is real, that he is inspired by a great vision, and that he is ready to put his life down for his vision.

When we depend on our emotional responses, we can be trapped by those forceful people who appear to be charismatic. But their only intention is to manipulate us for their self-interest. Real charisma is interested in the welfare of others to the degree that he can actually forget himself in service to others.

Some writers want us to think that they can teach people how to become charismatic. They say, for example, that a person must dress a certain way, behave a certain way, make eye contact, touch, use the voice in a certain way, and so on. Without denying that such advice may improve the personality and may create better contact if carried out in sincerity, the fact is that if a person has charisma, it does not matter how he dresses, how he talks, how he looks, or how he behaves because his charisma will make everything he does charismatic. Is this to say that all such advice is futile? In some sense, the answer is yes, if the suggestions are related to the personality.

Real charisma is developed only by activating virtues and spirituality. The Inner Fire in man must be kindled. Once this is accomplished, it will radiate out with greater magnetism and beauty. It will program all expressions of the man charismatically.

How do we develop this Inner Fire and kindle it?

- The first step is meditation.
- The second is to develop spiritual vision so that the entire person is attracted to that vision.
- The third step is to cultivate a path of sacrificial service dedicated to human welfare.
- Fourth is to forget about charisma and decide to serve people.
- Self-forgetfulness is the fifth way to release the Inner Fire.
- The sixth step is to cultivate the conviction that you are essentially a Divine Spark.
- The seventh is to realize that the One Self is in every living form.

Through actualizing these procedures, charisma is eventually developed — a charisma which will help a person draw more people into the orbit of his vision and evoke their essential Divinity to express Itself.

Permanent changes cannot come through cosmetics or through artificiality but only from inner resources.

Real charisma is not an imposition but the power that releases you from your psychic or emotional and mental prisons. Real charisma makes you free.

People talk about charisma as a power that makes a person attractive to others or makes people "spellbound" by the words and expressions of the charismatic person. But this is not true charisma. True charisma is not the interest you show toward the personalities of people or to their stories related to common problems or pleasures of humanity.

In real charisma you are put in touch through the charismatic person with the fires within you, with the fires of your dreams and visions. You are drawn out from your prisons, and you are freed in space where you can face infinity and you can decide to sail into infinity.

People with "personal magnetism" or sexiness, those who are demanding and imposing figures, are not truly charismatic but are people who control others with interest-associations and posthypnotic suggestions.

One need not be a spiritual leader or a religious person to be charismatic. Charisma is found in all fields of human endeavor. It expresses itself through words, mannerisms, dreams, visions, directions, and purposes. It manifests itself in the true knowledge that people have, in their wisdom, beauty, joy, health, skills, and creativity.

Charisma is psychic energy — the Holy Spirit. Once a person is charged, or filled, with such energy, he is charismatic.

Charisma is often viewed from the angle of what it does to others. But it must also be observed from the viewpoint of what it does to the one who is charismatic. Charisma attracts angelic beings to the person. Creative forces of the Universe make contact with him. Higher sources of inspiration touch him, and he begins to receive impressions that connect him to the symphony going on in every living form.

Thus, psychic energy, or charisma, becomes a bridge between man and the Universe — a communication network that develops from the initial instinctive response to a conscious and intuitional response to that network.

That is why we are told that psychic energy is the AUM which vibrates in all that exists, vitalizing and leading us to a concealed Purpose.

The energy of charisma is like an electromagnetic current that streams forth from the human Core, charging the network of the Golden Bridge and radiating out in the aura with beauty, energy, love, peace, and serenity.

22

Higher Sources of Treasures

In the Ageless Wisdom, we read about three suns. The highest one is called the Central Spiritual Sun, from which emanates all that exists in space. Then we have galactic suns, which are called the Heart of the Sun. Finally, we have solar suns, which are like the one we have in our solar system. All three of these suns are treasures of the Universe at their own level and in their own field of creation.

It is from these three suns that Light, Love, and Power (Truth, Goodness, and Beauty) emanate. These are distributed throughout the Universe through the agents of Light, Love, and Power.

There is a very close relationship between the stars and man; the stars are the future of man. Legend says that at one time each sun was a spark that traveled throughout millions of ages and eventually became a human being – then a planet, then gradually a sun, a galactic sun, and a part of the Central Spiritual Sun.

These suns, throughout millions and millions of lives, accumulated knowledge, experience, wisdom, and power as they lived in various relationships on various planes and turned into treasures of knowledge, light, love, power, and life.

When we speak about treasure, most people limit this concept by thinking about money, jewelry, gems, precious stones, antiques, and so on. Often these are parts of a treasure. But there are physical treasures, emotional treasures, mental treasures, Intuitional, Atmic, Monadic, and Divine Treasures. There are treasures related to Light, Compassion, and Love. There are treasures related to Willpower, Life, leadership, and rulership.

Every treasure is a condensation of light from one of the three suns. For example, emotions, thoughts, ideas, visions, and revelations are actually phenomena of sun rays. In each sun ray are condensed the wisdom, the principles, the life, and the laws of Nature. Until our devices are ready to interpret and translate these rays, they seem just to be rays of light. All come from the source of light, and all will return to that source of light through walking on the path of light as units of light.

In every human being, planet, solar system, and galaxy, there exist keys to unlock these treasures. For example, the human soul in man is the key to the sun; the Solar Angel in man is the key to the Heart of the Sun; and the Self — the Core of the human being — is the key to the Central Spiritual Sun.

Our planet also has three keys. One key is called the Tower, which is a key to the door of the Central Spiritual Sun. The next key is called the Hierarchy, which is the key to the treasury of the Heart of the Sun. The final key is the New Group of World Servers, which, taken as a group, is the key to the wisdom of our sun.

There are three keys and three treasuries. The three treasuries nourish and sustain all that exists within the visible and invisible Universe.

The highest treasury is the treasury from which shines forth the mysterious energy called Life Energy, Beauty, Glory, Power, Will, and Synthesis.

The second treasury is the treasury of Compassion, Unity, Love, and Wisdom.

The third treasury is Knowledge and Light.

The treasures we receive from the Central Spiritual Sun can be translated into human language as the Will behind the Purpose of Cosmic Existence and the streams of Life running through all that exists.

All the sages and scientists cannot exhaust the mystery of Life, Will, and Purpose. Only grains of knowledge are given to humanity from this Cosmic Treasury, and these grains are translated as

- Sacrificial Will
- Courage
- Steadfastness
- Fearlessness
- Leadership
- Peace
- Serenity
- Stability
- Equilibrium
- Purpose
- Synthesis
- Glory

- Solemnity
- Magnanimity
- The Laws of Spirit
- The Laws of Soul

These drops fall, or are brought down by Great Ones, to humanity from the Central Spiritual Sun. Each drop contains the Universe in itself, and as we evaluate these seeds in our life we slowly find the secret paths to contact occasionally that Cosmic Source of Treasure.

There is a thread that extends from the Central Spiritual Sun and anchors itself in the heart of each living form, from an atom to a galaxy. It is through this thread that the Central Spiritual Sun directs every living form throughout millions of lives back to Itself,

From Whom all things proceed;
To Whom all things return.

Thus, through this life-thread every form is programmed to return eventually to its Source, to be one with the Source, to reach the Treasury.

The Central Spiritual Sun in man — his Core, his True Self — must eventually come in contact with the Tower of the solar system and the galaxy and make a contact with the Central Spiritual Sun. Once such a communication line is established, the person, or the individuality, will turn into a Center of Life on the planet, radiating the power of the Central Spiritual Sun.

As we advance, we turn into a treasury in all senses: physically, emotionally, mentally, morally, and spiritually. We see this in the history of humanity in the examples of Great

Ones Who, after reaching a high level of beingness or self-actualization, demonstrated the Treasury in Their lives.

By sharing these treasures you increase them a thousand-fold. The sun increases its radiation as it shares its light, chemistry, and life with all its friends in the solar system — and beyond.

Nothing decreases through sharing. Nothing increases in taking. If only we could understand and accept this treasure and enrich our life with this treasure.

The Central Spiritual Sun can be reached through sacrifice. When we say "sacrifice," people think about cutting the necks of poor animals and offering them to the gods. Sacrifice is radiation of the most sacred that exists in man — his True Self, the spark of God. When this Sacred Diamond begins to shine out and stream forth Its rays through our thoughts, words, and actions, we say that we have become sacrificial. And as we sacrifice, we increase in our power, beauty, and glory.

The Central Spiritual Sun is the Sacrifice, just as every sun is a symbol of sacrifice.

The treasures hidden in the Heart of the Sun are very precious and without having drops or grains of such treasures, all would collapse in the Universe.

The most precious treasure hidden in the Core of the Heart of the Sun is called compassion. Compassion manifests through the Law of Attraction — Love. From the Heart of the Sun, compassion is radiated toward every heart, toward every form in the Universe.

Compassion is the source of unity, creativity, right relationship, and contact. It is the treasury of the Heart of the

Sun that holds together forms in existence, makes them increase and multiply, and develops right sensitivity toward the Central Spiritual Sun.

Human beings can use such a treasure, perhaps only as much as five percent. Five percent of these treasures can be translated into our language as

- Love
- Devotion
- Dedication
- Education in all its branches
- Cooperation
- Harmony
- Religion
- Patience
- Endurance
- Faithfulness
- Intuition
- Art
- Teaching
- The Laws of Psychic Energy
- The Laws of Holy Spirit
- The Laws of Matter

The path toward this sun passes through our hearts and develops the above precious stones. All art objects that we have are the result of one drop from this treasury. Of course, this treasury shares its treasures with mineral, vegetable, and also animal kingdoms according to their capacity to receive, transform, and change.

A human being approaches this treasure through his Inner Guide, through mastering his life and contacting the center which we call the Hierarchy. The Hierarchy is the Lotus which blossoms on the currents of the energy coming from the Heart of the Sun.

The third treasury is hidden in the Core of our sun, which is the source of prana and light. Rays coming from this sun are interpreted or translated in the human consciousness as

- Enlightenment
- Service
- Tolerance
- Sincerity
- Love-Wisdom
- Divine Indifference
- Accuracy
- Science
- Rhythm

The three suns are also reflected in the system of our chakras. The head center corresponds to the Central Spiritual Sun. The heart center corresponds to the Heart of the Sun. The throat chakra corresponds to the sun. And as we develop these centers, as they unfold, they put us in contact with the corresponding spheres.

Each ray of the sun carries within itself the total knowledge of our solar system. If one day we discover how to translate these rays, we will not need to search for knowledge. A single ray will reveal to us whatever we want to know.

Every beam that comes from the sun carries out the wisdom that is accumulated in the soul of the Entity who ensouls the sun as Its body. But human beings, in relation to such a treasury, are like ants walking upon the most precious treasures, occupied by the urge to search for a piece of food.

Our planet with all its kingdoms is only a handful of treasure given by our sun. Imagine one beam of light extending from the sun as a hand holding in itself our globe with all that exists on it.

One may ask, "If the sun is all knowledge, wisdom, and energy, why then is there war, famine, diseases, and destruction on our globe?" The answer is "because of stupidity." Through our stupidity we exploited the planet and each other and created artificial walls between ourselves and the planet, between ourselves and the rest of humanity, and we reacted to the wisdom of the sun instead of responding to it.

The essence of everything is in the physical sun. The Archetypes of all living forms are in the Heart of the Sun. The direction of every form, the map of every form, is hidden in the Central Spiritual Sun.

Once Christ said, "Ask for treasure with faith and in My Name." This is a very condensed expression and it means, "Tell our Father that it is Me in you who is asking for treasure, and that the person asking for treasure on My behalf will receive the treasure and bring it to Me." This means that the treasure will only be used for the purpose that Christ has in His Heart.

We can respond to the treasuries of the sun and to the higher suns by trying to live a life of harmony with all that exists. We polluted the air, the water, the soil of the planet;

we destroyed the rivers, forests, animals, and birds — and we still hope that we can continue whatever we have been doing. But unless we start creating harmony between us and all things that exist, we may destroy all that we have built throughout the ages and end our lives in global suicide.

Harmonious relationship will be established only by annihilating the barriers that we constructed between us and the rest of the living forms. This is what purification essentially is.

People are poor if they do not have treasures from these three suns. Christ said, "Collect treasures in heaven." This is such a precious wisdom. The three suns are not only treasures but are also banks in which you save your treasures to use and share on the path of your solar and Cosmic evolution.

We deposit treasures into our sun by living a life of light, truth, righteousness, justice, and sacrificial service to educate and enlighten human beings. Everything that you think, talk, and do in the light, for the light is a jewel which goes directly to the treasury of the sun — where it accumulates and draws interest that is used by the bank as loans in an emergency for other people. Many lives will pass, and your path toward the Cosmos will be built by the treasury you deposit in the solar bank.

We also can put treasures in the Heart of the Sun every time we truly love without expectation, devote ourselves to a great task, live under the laws of the soul, create harmony between people, and spread understanding. Wherever your treasure is, there your heart is, and in the darkest hours of your life you will witness the help standing on your threshold from your solar bank.

Every time we live in hatred, greed, fear, anger, jealousy, revenge, or stupidity, we waste the treasures of the Universe and create starving conditions in the world. Our life is a jewel. We must multiply our treasures to keep harmonious relations with all treasuries in the Universe.

Any time you bury a treasure and do not use it or share it, it will rot and you will become indebted to the treasury.

Once a young woman told me, "I have a treasure and I want to share it with humanity." "What is that treasure, " I asked. "My singing," she said. This person went all over the world, throughout the United States, to Russia, and to China. Many people came to hear her sing. When she returned to the United States, I met her and she was the most happy woman. "I will share my treasure with all whom I can," she said to me. She was a treasure herself.

We add to our treasures in the Central Spiritual Sun by living a life of supreme sacrifice, a life of leadership, a life filled with the fire of purpose. These are the jewels which you can add to the treasury of the Central Spiritual Sun.

Everyone who knows how to sacrifice, how to lead, how to live a purposeful life is himself a treasure. How imperative it is to make ourselves into treasures and even treasuries! Is your body a treasury of energy and health? Is your heart a treasury of love and compassion? Is your mind a treasury of knowledge? Is your soul a treasury of virtue? Until we become a treasure, we will not have the right to enter into the treasury. The treasuries do not accumulate cabbages — but only treasures.

There are great officers or messengers who serve as communication lines between treasuries. For example, between the Central Spiritual Sun and the Heart of the Sun there are many lofty Beings Who are lives of the Greater Zodiac, such as the Great Bear, Sirius, Pleiades. And Great Avatars are lines between Them and the Heart of the Sun.

There are other Great Beings Who connect the Heart of the Sun and our sun. They are zodiacal Beings and some Spirits and Avatars like the Avatar of Synthesis, the Spirit of Peace, and the Spirit of Resurrection Who through our Hierarchy try to inspire humanity with new visions.

The Avatar of Synthesis is bringing to us the jewel of synthesis, the jewel of the New Era, to inspire all galactic and solar beings by this treasure.

The Spirit of Peace brings the jewel of peace to all beings in Cosmic space.

The Spirit of Resurrection is bringing to us the jewel of striving to get out of our physical, moral, mental, emotional, and spiritual graves. The graves of materialism, totalitarianism, and separatism must be left behind by experiencing resurrection into a new dimension of consciousness.

There are other Beings Who bring treasures from the sun to our planet. They are called Divine Contemplatives, Those Who connect the Father's House to humanity. They are Great Ones such as Lord Buddha, Christ, Zoroaster, and Hercules.

Thus the Central Spiritual Sun, the Heart of the Sun, the sun, the planet, and each form of life are connected to each other with a spiritual thread.

We must learn about the existence of treasuries and accept the treasures we find all around us with deepest gratitude and with deepest humility based on self-forgetfulness, harmlessness, and right speech.

No one will be allowed to enter into the first treasury except through self-forgetfulness.

No one will be able to enter into the second treasury except through harmlessness.

No one will be able to enter into the third treasury without right speech — without manifesting pure light.

If we violate this formula, we will use all treasures against our own survival. If we misuse the treasures given to us, we will be punished by the Laws of Life. But if we use the treasures and multiply them to increase the bliss in the Universe, we will reach our Cosmic destination.

Man essentially is bliss; he originated from the source of bliss. On the path of involution, this drop of bliss became matter — and eventually took human form. We forgot about Home, as the prodigal son did for a while, but there is a thread in our heart that extends to us from Home. Eventually we will find the Path leading Home.

The head, heart, and throat centers are translators of the rays coming from the sun, from the Heart of the Sun, and from the Central Spiritual Sun. As these centers unfold and organize, they become able to draw in more treasures from these rays in terms of knowledge, love, and willpower.

Without our sun, these centers will not operate. Animals cannot enjoy creative thinking, knowledge, compassionate relationships, willpower, or direction because they do not have these centers. Only their sex, solar plexus, and base of spine centers translate the rays of our sun; and they are used for breeding, as various instincts, and as the power to hunt and survive.

All of these treasures are given to all living things everywhere because every advancing soul on the path to perfection must demonstrate an ability to give and an ability to create things that fit progressively.

But there is a treasure-key which unlocks all the treasures of the Universe. It is called the Holy Spirit, psychic energy, or even wisdom.

It is most essential to have this energy because only through this energy can a person enjoy all the treasures and use them properly and goal-fittingly. Only right usage of treasures increases them and keeps the user in a condition in which he is always capable of enjoying them and using them for his own development.

Without psychic energy, treasures can be used for self-destructive ends and for the retardation of our progress.

Meditation on the Sun:

1. Observe one minute of total silence.

2. Calm your body. Fill your heart with love. Fill your mind with joy.

3. Imagine yourself sitting in light.

4. Visualize that you are entering into the sun, and let the sun purify all the darkness that exists in your threefold being. Heal your vehicles by disbursing all that exists as pollution in your being. Give yourself to the sun and see yourself transforming and becoming a transparent form of light.

lution in your being. Give yourself to the sun and see yourself transforming and becoming a transparent form of light.

5. Now visualize yourself entering into the Heart of the Sun up in the sky, and fly to that sun. As you enter into it, visualize yourself reaching the center as a shining sun. Let your heart be filled with the fire of compassion. In the fiery sphere of that sun, visualize raising your hands, and say:

"In all my life, I will think in Compassion, speak in Compassion, act in Compassion. No hatred or separativeness will exist within me. I will be one with the fire of Compassion. And so let it be."

Now feel your heart embracing the whole Universe.

6. Visualize the Central Spiritual Sun in ruby fire, and with one of Its rays, travel into It. Kneel down within the Sun and say:

"My Lord and my Source, from Whom every thing proceeds, to Whom every thing returns, accept my striving and aspiration. I will try in everything and everywhere to stand within Your Will. Your Will be done throughout my life, and let me be a beam of Your Will throughout my life."

7. OM. OM. OM.

Index

B

H

I

M

N

T

U

V

About the Author

Torkom Saraydarian (1917 – 1997) was born in Asia Minor. Since childhood he was trained in the Teachings of the Ageless Wisdom.

He visited monasteries, ancient temples, and mystery schools in order to find the answers to his questions about the mystery of man and the Universe.

He lived with Sufis, dervishes, Christian mystics, and masters of temple music and dance. His musical training included the violin, piano, oud, cello, and guitar. It took long years of discipline and sacrifice to absorb the Ageless Wisdom from its true sources. Meditation became a part of his daily life, and service a natural expression of his soul.

Torkom Saraydarian dedicated his entire life to the service of his fellow man. His writings and lectures and music show his total devotion to the higher principles, values, and laws that are present in all world religions and philosophies. These works represent a synthesis of the best and most beautiful in the sacred culture of the world. His works enrich the foundational thinking on which man can construct his Future.

Torkom Saraydarian wrote a large number of books, many of which have been published. All of his books will continue to be published and distributed. A few have been translated into Armenian, German, Italian, Spanish, Portuguese, Greek, Dutch, and Danish.

He left a rich legacy of writings and musical compositions for all of humanity to enjoy and benefit from for many years to come.

Visit our web site at www.tsgfoundation.org for interviews and additional information on Torkom Saraydarian.

Other Books by Torkom Saraydarian

- The Ageless Wisdom
- The Aura
- Battling Dark Forces
- The Bhagavad Gita
- Breakthrough to Higher Psychism
- Buddha Sutra — A Dialogue with the Glorious One
- Challenge for Discipleship
- Christ, The Avatar of Sacrificial Love
- A Commentary on Psychic Energy
- Cosmic Shocks
- Cosmos in Man
- The Creative Fire
- The Creative Sound
- Dialogue with Christ (2nd ed.)
- Dynamics of Success
- Education as Transformation, Vol. I
- Education as Transformation, Vol. II
- The Eyes of Hierarchy—How the Masters Watch and Help Us
- Flame of Beauty, Culture, Love, Joy
- The Flame of the Heart
- From My Heart — Volume I (Poetry)
- Glossary, A Concordance of Torkom Saraydarian's Works
- Hiawatha and the Great Peace
- The Hidden Glory of the Inner Man
- I Was
- Joy and Healing
- Karma and Reincarnation
- Leadership Vol. I
- Leadership Vol. II
- Leadership Vol. III
- Leadership Vol. IV
- Leadership Vol. V
- Legend of Shamballa
- The Mystery of Self-Image
- The Mysteries of Willpower
- New Dimensions in Healing
- Obsession and Possession
- Olympus World Report… The Year 3000
- One Hundred Names of God
- Other Worlds
- The Psyche and Psychism
- The Psychology of Cooperation and Group Consciousness
- The Purpose of Life
- The Science of Becoming Oneself
- The Science of Meditation
- The Sense of Responsibility in Society
- Sex, Family, and the Woman in Society, *2nd ed.*
- The Solar Angel
- Spiritual Regeneration
- Spring of Prosperity
- The Subconscious Mind and the Chalice
- Symphony of the Zodiac
- Talks on Agni
- Talks on Agni, Vol. 2
- Talks on Agni, Vol. 3
- Thought & the Glory of Thinking
- Transformation
- Triangles of Fire
- Unusual Court
- Woman, Torch of the Future
- The Year 2000 & After

For all of Torkom Saraydarian's latest books and creative works visit our website at www.tsgfoundation.org

Booklets

- The Art of Visualization — Simply Presented
- The Chalice in Agni Yoga Literature
- Cornerstones of Health
- A Daily Discipline of Worship
- Discipleship in Action
- Daily Spiritual Striving
- Earrings for Business People
- Earthquakes and Disasters — What the Ageless Wisdom Tells Us
- Fiery Carriage and Drugs
- Hierarchy and the Plan
- How to Find Your Level of Meditation
- Inner Blooming
- Irritation — The Destructive Fire
- Mental Exercises
- Nachiketas
- New Beginnings
- Practical Spirituality
- Prayers, Mantrams and Invocations (now includes *Five Great Mantrams of the New Age*)
- Questioning Traveler and Karma
- Saint Sergius
- Synthesis

Booklets

(Excerpts and Compilations)

- Angels and Devas
- Courage
- First Steps Toward Freedom
- Prayers, Mantrams, and Invocations

Family Series Booklets

- Duties of Grandparents
- Cooperation
- Family Relations
- For Men
- For Women
- Ideal Marriage
- Responsibility
- Responsibilities of Fathers
- Responsibilities of Mothers
- Success
- The Heart of Your Partner
- Women as Torchbearers

Video and Audio Lectures

- The Seven Rays Interpreted
- Why Drugs Are Dangerous
- Complete list of lecture video and audio tapes by author available at **www.tsgfoundation.org**

Music

- A Touch of Heart (CD only)
- Dance of the Zodiac
- Far Horizons
- Fire Blossom
- Infinity
- Lao Tse
- Light Years Ahead
- Lily in Tibet
- Misty Mountain
- Piano Composition
- Rainbow
- Spirit of My Heart
- Sun Rhythms
- Tears of My Joy
- Toward Freedom
- 1994 Annual Convention Special Edition — Synthesizer Music

About the Publisher

T.S.G. Publishing Foundation, Inc. is a non-profit, tax exempt organization. Founded on November 30, 1987 in Los Angles, California, it relocated to Cave Creek, Arizona on January 1, 1994.

Our purpose is to be a pathway for self-transformation. We are fully devoted to publishing, teaching, and distributing the creative works of Torkom Saraydarian.

Our bookstore in Cave Creek and our online bookstore at our web site www.tsgfoundation.org offers the complete collection of the creative works of Torkom Saraydarian for sale and distribution.

Our newsletter *Outreach* contains thought-provoking articles and is available both in print and from our website with free email notification.

We also conduct weekly classes, special training seminars, and home study meditation courses.

The Torkom Saraydarian University

Torkom Saraydarian dreamed of a training center, often calling it the **University**, where men and women can be trained in the theory and application of Higher Principles and Values of the Ageless Wisdom. He called such higher education "Aquarian Education" and continuously encouraged his students to form such an institution in the future.

There is an increasing need for leadership in the field of esoteric knowledge. More and more people are becoming disillusioned with the teachings given to them by opportunists, by people who have good intentions but are full of glamors and vanities, or by people who want to use the Teaching as a business to raise money.

Great damage is done to people who approach the Teaching with sincerity in their heart and are caught in groups, institutions, or organizations that are only for social activities or that function as traps for exploitation. Some of these searchers gradually forget about their quest and adapt themselves to their environment. Some of them totally suppress their aspiration and spiritual striving because of their disillusionment. Only a small percentage, through discrimination, continue their search to find the proper field where they can grow and serve.

The number of true searchers is increasing. We must prepare ourselves to meet their need and at the same time safeguard ourselves from the dangers of falling into vanities, glamors, or of using the searchers for our own interests.

Torkom Saraydarian, *Leadership I,* p. 16.

Our first training courses were launched in September 2000. We have classes on site as well as by correspondence. For information on classes and online registration visit our website at www.torkomsaraydarianuniversity.org or write to us.

Torkom Saraydarian Book Publishing Fund

Torkom Saraydarian dedicated his entire life to serving others in their spiritual growth. At the time of his passing, more than 100 manuscripts had been written and prepared for publication. This work represents a seamless tapestry of Wisdom and we are dedicated to publishing the entire collection.

He had the unique wisdom and dedication to write all of these magnificent books in one lifetime. Now it is our turn to do the work. Together we can make his dream a reality and bring his legacy to fruition.

We depend on contributions for the publishing of the books. A special fund, *The Torkom Saraydarian Book Publishing Fund* has been established for the completion of this legacy. Contact us for details about the *Book Fund* and an update regarding remaining manuscripts.

As we go to press with this book we have at least 75 titles not yet published! We need your help to release these treasuries of Wisdom.

You can contribute funds for an entire book, or give any amount you wish on a continuous basis or a one-time contribution.

Thank you for your loving and continuous support.

Ordering Information

All of Torkom's creative works and TSG's products are available for purchase at www.tsgfoundation.org

If you do not have internet access you may write to the publisher for additional information regarding:

— Free catalog of author's books and music tapes

— Complete list of lecture tapes and videos ($2 postage for each list - available for free on the website)

— Placement on mailing list for continuous updates

— A free copy of our newsletter *Outreach* (latest edition, plus archived copies available on the website)

— **Join our Book Club at no charge. (Receive a 20% discount with each new release by Torkom Saraydarian. Each new book is mailed to you automatically as soon as it is released.) Send us a written approval to include you in the Book Club.**

Additional copies of *Dynamics of the Soul*

U.S. $25.00

Contact us for shipping and handling rates. For international orders please indicate whether you want surface or air.

T.S.G. Publishing Foundation, Inc.

P.O. Box 7068

Cave Creek, AZ 85327–7068

United States of America

TEL: (480) 502–1909

FAX: (480) 502–0713

E-Mail: info@tsgfoundation.org

For additional information about the publisher, visit the website at: www.tsgfoundation.org